We dedicate this book to all the spirits in Cookstown who came forward to talk to us and all the store managers, employees, citizens and business owners in Cookstown who graciously allowed us to investigate their properties and shared their stories. We also dedicate this book to medium Sheila Trecartin who communicated with the spirits and to Joan McLean for her in depth historical research on the buildings. This book would not be possible without them.

ISBN 978-1-77136-320-4
Printed and bound in Canada by Art Bookbindery

Table of Contents

Introduction

I first became aware of my sixth sense when I was around 12 years old. I would remember dreams and then something similar would happen from the dream in my waking life. I would think of a situation and have a good or bad feeling about it. I believe everyone has this "intuition". Even animals do. They have a sense of when something is about to occur. Why would God not instill that in us? Some might call this coincidence or luck when we think, say or dream of something that happens but I believe there are no coincidences.

Later in life, I found myself knowing when spirit or residual energy was around me. I would feel light headed, like something was interfering with my energy. I would feel it mostly in antique stores as they are filled with residual energy but the feeling was the strongest when there were actual spiritual energies around me. I would have a never-ending head rush until I left the area. Some spirits don't give off a lot of energy and some do so the intensity of my head rush was based on the energy of the spirit.

After having our second child, our little house in Churchill, Ontario was just not big enough for our growing family. We decided that we would like to move to a bigger house in a small community within walking distance of a school. On many occasions, before the kids were born, my husband and I would go antiquing in Cookstown. It always felt like we stepped back in time as many of the buildings still had their original charm and character. We knew that we wanted to live here.

Cookstown began as a crossroads in 1825. It was the intersection of four townships: Innisfil, West Gwillimbury, Tecumseth and Essa. A settlement then grew from this junction. In 1826, the Perry family built a log cabin on the northeast corner which was also a rest stop for weary travellers on route to Barrie. It became known as Perry's Corners. It was also noted that there were five mud huts in the settlement.

After the Perry family moved on, the Dixon family came to the northwest corner and built a home and tavern. The name of the settlement was then known as Dixon's Corners.

In 1830, Mr. Thomas Cooke came from Stewart Town and bought 600 acres of farm land. In 1847 he registered the land as lots and sold them. He did so under the name of Cooke's Town. The name was later changed to Cookstown.

Our family has enjoyed the move to Cookstown. We attend family events like the Wing Ding town wide yard sale and the 'Light up the Night' Christmas parade. I even joined the Cookstown Chamber of Commerce. I couldn't think of a better place to raise a family, even if it comes with ghostly visitors. As a graphic artist, I love to do paintings and artwork with a spiritual theme so this was a perfect town for me.

The idea of this book came to me while I was sitting in on a meeting for the Cookstown Chamber of Commerce. They decided to have the meeting in an historical building, a store called "Thru the Grapevine" at 21 Queen Street. When I first moved to Cookstown, I shopped at this store and went upstairs only to come down and tell the owner that I believed they had a spirit. The owner stated that another woman once told her that there was a kind female spirit upstairs as well. During our meeting I did feel the spirit come down for a visit. I thought to myself how nice it would be to draw business to the town by having a ghost walk but what would we talk about? Then the idea of a book came to mind. Over the years, I had heard of several haunted sites in Cookstown but no one had ever bothered to gather these stories and put them together in a book before.

The next day I emailed Cate Crow. I met Cate at Cherry Valley Spiritual Healing Retreat in Thornton. This site is a supernatural hot spot with ghosts, native spirits, angels and even animal spirits. We clicked right away. Cate was a former History and English teacher and I knew she loved to write about spiritual topics, especially about ghosts. Cate had already written a ghost book for Black Creek Pioneer Village, "The Ghosts of Black Creek", which was featured in Canadian author Terry Boyle's book, "Ghostly Historic Sites, Inns and Miracles" and "More Ontario Ghost Stories" by Maria Da Silva and Andrew Hind. She started the ghost walk at Black Creek Pioneer Village. She wrote spiritual articles for the Innisfil Scope, the New Tecumseh Times and the Shelburne Free Press newspapers. "The Ghosts of Simcoe County" was one of the articles she submitted to these newspapers. Cate had also appeared on Roger's Talk of the Town television show to talk about the haunted Museum on the Boyne in Alliston and Roger's Daytime television show to talk about the spirits at Cherry Valley Farm in Thornton. I emailed her the idea and by coincidence the time stamp on the email was 11:11am. It is said that this is a sign from the angels. Cate took the sign seriously and we joined together to write this book. Cate can also sense spirits in her own way although she describes it as more of a pressure feeling and she can often pick up emotions through it. We seem to feel out the same spaces and can sense when a spirit is around. However, neither of us have such strong psychic abilities as Sheila Trecartin of Ultimate Healing Concepts in Cookstown. Sheila has been actively speaking to and seeing the spirit world since she was a child. She is also a gifted healer and animal communicator. We must thank Sheila for all her help in confirming our finds for this book which further proves the existence of life after death.

Amy Woodcock

1 Queen Street
Courtney's Story

Courtney currently lives in one of the apartments above the ice cream store at 1 Queen Street. The original building was made out of logs in the 1830's and was a store. It was one of the first stores in Cookstown. From 1922 until 1962 it was owned by the Monkman family. They sold hardware, fencing supplies and radios. From 1947 on, Don Monkman owned a garage and Imperial Oil Esso station at the site. It remained a gas station even after it changed owners.

Courtney claimed that she was a "sensitive" and stated in her apartment she has seen shadow figures as well as a male spirit and child spirit. She saw the male spirit as clear as day and described him as tall, slender with a thin mustache, brown hair and wearing coveralls. She said he appeared to come from the 1920's era. He appeared to her for 30 seconds to a minute while she was on the sofa and then disappeared again. She said she felt it must have been a former store owner who once lived above the shop. This was possibly someone from the Monkman family who owned the building in the 1920's.

Image courtesy of the Joan McLean Collection, ourstoriesinnisfil.ca

Courtney also claimed that every time her roommate's 4 year old child came to the apartment, she saw and talked to another spirit who was a little boy. At one time, the 4 year old girl blurted out, "you should get a haircut!"

Medium Sheila Trecartin from Ultimate Healing Concepts in Cookstown was able to confirm a young lady spirit in the top left room. She once lived there with her husband in the 1940's. After losing a child, they had 3 more children. The child they lost is possibly the spirit the 4 year old girl sees. Sheila picked up a "ding ding" sound, the kind of sound you once heard when a tire rolled over a bell so a car could be serviced and get gas. It could have also been the sound of a store bell indicating they had a customer. She also picked up whiskey jugs with horses out front in the early 1800's. It is very possible that this site was once the location of a saloon given the early history of the area. Sheila did not pick up on a male spirit but she said he could have been a visiting spirit and not a ghost who haunts the building.

Across the street from the ice cream parlour, Sheila picked up four spirits who came from different locations around the town.

The first spirit was a woman who was connected to the Old Chestnut Inn. She said she met a man here and ended up staying in Cookstown until she died in childbirth at the age of 34. Sheila described her as wearing a green hat with a feather and an emerald green dress. The female spirit said this spot was once a stop off point for the stage coach.

Sheila picked up the spirit of another older man who once owned a bakery in town. There was once a bakery on Church Street which was built in 1874. The bakery was in operation for well over 100 years. Sheila also picked up another male spirit who was a grounds keeper for the bakery in the late 1800's.

Finally, Sheila picked up the spirit of an 18 year old girl with brown hair who committed suicide. She was wearing t-shirt and jeans. The girl said she was from the area and hung out here in the 1980's and 90's at a restaurant that sold pizza and also a bar. She spoke about a boy named William and a man named Matthew. She had a hard life and was heavily into drugs. She also said she was punishing herself by staying and did not want to cross over.

Prior to living in her apartment above the ice cream parlour, Courtney lived in an apartment two blocks down on Queen Street from January 2009 to September 2013. The first building on this site was erected in the mid 1800's. It was later torn down at the turn of the last century. The current house was then built in the early 1900's.

Courtney said this house came with 3 spirits; a child, a middle aged man and something horrible in the basement. She said the entity in the basement would slam doors, attack her, push her, pull her hair and scratch her while she was doing laundry. Courtney stated she was colour blind and could not see the colour red but for some strange reason she could see red eyes on this dark figure. She also told us when her docile cat went into the basement, she would hiss and freak out at whatever the entity was. At one point Courtney had to lock the cat in the bathroom for an hour to get it to calm down from whatever it saw. She claimed that one area of the basement by the cellar was particularly bad.

Courtney told us that the man who owned the property at one time found 3 to 4 inverted pentagrams in the basement. Obviously, someone was into some kind of dark cult or practice and brought this poltergeist energy into the house. It is the same reason Ouija boards should not be played with. You can unknowingly invite this kind of dark energy into your house as well.

Courtney thought this entity was confined to the basement until she was sleeping in bed upstairs one night and felt something pull her pajama pant leg up. After that, she stated the blanket flew off the bed and across the room. Items also flew off the mantle and were thrown at her. In the living room heavy items were moved and at one point the swinging door to the kitchen slammed shut and it took 10 minutes to get the door to open. Courtney said even her ex-military friend would not stay in the house alone and had to sleep with the lights on at all times.

At one point, Courtney had a paranormal group in to investigate. Apart from the dark entity in the basement, they claimed there was the spirit of a middle aged minister who was attached to a church in town on the main floor of the house. Courtney said she could often smell brandy or liquor in what was once the parlour. Hopefully, the minister is helping to keep the dark entity in the basement at bay!

Finally, Courtney mentioned a child spirit upstairs in the house who liked to knock on walls. "You could often hear her walking around", Courtney said. The lady who lived above Courtney at the time had a granddaughter the age of six who would play with the child spirit. She would carry on lengthy conversations with her and play games with her.

Medium Sheila Trecartin had the following to say about the house 2 weeks before we did the interview, "I know the place that you refer too. I have always said that it was terribly haunted. There is a presence in there that does not want to let go of that house. It does not have a good feel to it at all."

Two other members of the community told us the following:
"I walked by that house and I had shivers. That was before I heard the stories."

"I live across the street from this house. There have been many people who have moved in and out of that house in the past few years!"

That is certainly understandable.

We received another email from a man named Bob who wrote us the following:
"I lived in this home for 8 years, from 1978-86, and I hate to rain on the parade but honest to God there was absolutely no paranormal events or haunting of any kind that I experienced when I was there and as a kid I combed every inch and corner of the place, from the basement to the attic - nothing, nada, zip, no haunting, sorry to disappoint."

We were not disappointed. This just revealed that the pentagrams were placed in the basement sometime between

1986, after Bob moved out of the house, and January 2009 when Courtney moved in. It is possible that the minister has taken up residence in the home because of the dark entity. It is also possible that the child may be a visiting spirit only and is not actually haunting the building.

We have purposely not given the address of this home to protect the privacy of the current owners.

9 Queen Street
The Old Chestnut Inn

Built in 1865, this building was originally a store with a dwelling attached. To the right of the building there was an extension that was used as both an inn and a rooming house at different times. The store changed hands until 1924 when it was destroyed by fire. Once rebuilt, there was a barbershop and billiard's room on the east side of the building and a restaurant on the west side. In 1976, new owners bought the place and turned it into the Chestnut Inn. The Inn had a dining room that would seat 40 and a dinner theatre. The new owners also had an extension built onto the back of the building that held a reception room with a stage and bar. The Chestnut Inn

Image courtesy of the Cookstown Women's Institute, Tweedsmuir History

closed in 1993.

The Ontario and Toronto Ghosts and Hauntings Research Society have received the following reports on The Old Chestnut Inn and have published them on their website:

"I know of a place in Cookstown, just off the 400 at the highway 89 cut off. It used to be a restaurant. It has been said that there have been many sightings of a small girl coming down the stairs."
and
"I used to work in The Chestnut Inn and just so you know, the one that is famous for going down the stairs is a woman, not a little girl. The staff refers to her as Catherine. In the upstairs windows on some occasions, you can see the figure of a woman in black in the window. There is the sound of a little girl's laughter in the upstairs bedrooms as well. The worst place is in the basement. Apparently, at one time, there was a man who used to live in the basement. He was a little mentally challenged & was terrified of the dark. The first corner that you come to in the basement is where he used to try to hide from the "monsters" in the dark. When you pass by this area, your heart begins to pound like it is going to jump out of your chest. There have been some sensitives/mediums go through there in the past. There is said to be over 35 spirits there. If you drive by at night, sometimes you can see a man in the upstairs window. Although it is hard not to look at it at night, it seems to draw you in and make you look."

While we were interviewing Kim Turtscher at the old train station, she told us she knew someone who once worked at the building when it was the Old Chestnut Inn. She said different staff members saw a little girl on the stairs and a woman. One psychic said the little girl died of a sickness and was looking for her mommy. The psychic also picked up on other children and an abused woman upstairs, a man on the main floor who once tended bar in the 19th century and a woman in the kitchen who liked to bake. She picked up a simple minded man in the basement who tended to the boiler and stables and another man who was the night watchman.

Ghost Authors Maria da Silva and Andrew Hind published the following report on the Old Chestnut Inn in the Barrie Advance on October 27, 2006:

The Old Chestnut Inn in Cookstown is, according to some former staff and patrons, haunted by several restless ghosts. In fact, if psychics are to be believed, reservations are definitely in order at this quaint restaurant; after all, with as many as 35 errant spirits enjoying the timeless hospitality and fine food, table space must be limited.

Only a few of these ghosts make their presence known on a regular basis, two of whom were participants in a story of such tragic proportions it would have made Shakespeare proud.

The most commonly seen apparition is that of a beautiful

young woman, typically seen standing forlornly atop the stairs leading to the second-floor bed-and-breakfast rooms. The staff has taken to calling this tragic figure "Catherine", but somehow it stuck.

Local lore says that "Catherine", or whatever her name really was, came from a well-to-do family who, at some point in the late 19th century, owned and resided in the building. Catherine fell hopelessly in love with a dashing young man in town, but her father hated the notion. It seems the suitor wasn't deemed good enough for his beloved daughter.

Father and daughter argued frequently and loudly. It pained Catherine that the two men she loved couldn't both be a part of her life. She refused to choose between them, and continued to secretly see her beloved.

Then the unthinkable happened. Unwed Catherine was with child. In Victorian society, a scandal such as this could ruin a family. Her father was furious when he discovered her secret.

Everything he had built over his decades in town - the business, the sterling reputation, a position amongst the elite of society - could be destroyed by this one blight. He wouldn't have his life's work ruined in such a fashion. His reason clouded with anger, he decided to save his reputation even if it meant losing his daughter.

One morning, Catherine walked from the bedroom to come down for breakfast. Just as Catherine was about to descend the stairs, she felt a push from behind. The fall was lethal.

Though it was easy enough for Catherine's father to rid himself of scandal, it was not so easy to rid himself of his daughter. A free-spirited soul in life, she became even more restless in death.

Not long after her passing, Catherine began appearing again. And she continues to do so. Her spirit appears atop the staircase and then reenacts her fatal fall.

Waitresses busy with their tasks will occasionally hear the gut-wrenching sound of someone falling down the staircase. But when they run to investigate, they never find a body crumpled on the floor. In fact, they never find anybody at all.

On at least one occasion, Catherine was spotted standing atop the stairs, her mournful gaze looking down at the very spot where she died a century early. Within a blink of the eye, she vanished.

But this sad, despondent young woman isn't the only ghostly denizen of the Old Chestnut Inn to make its presence known. There's a dark, oppressive energy on the second floor that psychics say comes from a man haunted by guilt and anger. Passersby at night also claim to have seen the dark outline of a man framed in the upstairs window, a figure that sends shivers down one's spine and yet draws one's eyes like a moth to a flame. A common theory is that this soul is actually Catherine's father.

The foul deeds - assuming they took place - that led to the haunting of the Chestnut Inn occurred a century ago, and yet interest in the tragedy is strong. Perhaps it is this fascination that ties the melancholy spirit of Catherine to the spot where her earthly life ended?

The current owners of the building did not want to be investigated for ghosts so we were not able to confirm or deny these stories. As a result, we can only report on what we have heard about the Old Chestnut Inn in the past. The current owners did say that they have never experienced ghostly phenomenon in the building and state it is not haunted.

The Sheep Mercantile Co. owned by Monique Marshall and The Olde Bulldog Beanery owned by Philip Carver and Christine Fielding were recently opened at this location.

10 Queen Street
Cabo Clothing Store

Built in 1876 this landmark opened as a general store and pretty much stayed that way until 1984. The general store sold anything from food to clothing. In 1889 it was known as the "Fireproof House" as it was made of brick with an iron roof and had two fire doors. A lot of fires occurred on Queen Street and this building certainly stood the test of time.

In 1929, the back of the store was occupied by a lawyer, Mr. Duncan McCuaig, the father of the former mayor of Barrie, Janice Laking. The back room also has a large safe as the building may have at one time been a bank. Upstairs housed a millinery business that made the most beautiful hats. In 1984, it became an antique store and today it is a high end clothing store for women called Cabo. Cabo is owned by Michelle Malchuk who told us if there was a ghost in the store, it was upstairs and it was friendly. We went up to the second level and were immediately drawn into the front room. Sheila picked up the spirit of a woman whom she described as a "flapper" type from the 1920's. This friendly spirit talked about parties and entertainment happening at the hotel next door. That would have been the Mansion Hotel which burned to the ground in 1939. The spirit said a middle aged man owned this building and would get women to wine and dine visiting male guests. They were told to please the men to make money for his business. She said he would sit at a table downstairs eating steak while they entertained upstairs. At that point, the spirit of the man that the flapper worked for came forth and insisted that while he owned this building, the entertainment of the men by the ladies took place in his house.

Image courtesy of the Cookstown Women's Institute, Tweedsmuir History

In the 1920's which was the date given by the "flapper", the Cabo building was a general store with a hat making business upstairs owned by Lila Graham, a respectable business woman. It is unlikely that Lila used her hat store for the entertainment of men. We had to wonder at that point if the flapper was actually from the burned down hotel or another building and haunted this building instead.

As Sheila stated, "Ghosts will inhabit other buildings if the building they did inhabit is no longer there. They stay where they like or come and go as they like. Spirits are not confined to a location unless they are stuck and in a loop." The flapper was not stuck and could come and go as she pleased. Perhaps, the flapper frequented Lila Graham's store and bought her hats there when she was alive in the 1920's.

In researching the history of the building, it was discovered that there was a home between Cabo and Will Silk's. The history book states that the people who lived in that house owned "the store to the East", which would have been the Cabo building. It is very possible that this was the house the male spirit owned and this house was the place where the flapper spirit and other women entertained and wined and dined men for his business while he sat downstairs and ate in his kitchen.

The Mansion Hotel was also called The Wellington and The Lewis Hotel. It burned 3 times, once in 1877, again in 1933, and finally in 1939. The brick Clock Store building can be seen in this picture. Beside it is Eby & Co. Merchant Tailors before it was destroyed by fire in 1939.

Image courtesy of the Cookstown Women's Institute, Tweedsmuir History

The Mansion Hotel before it burned down.

Queen Street
The Old Queen's Hotel

Image courtesy of the Cookstown Women's Institute, Tweedsmuir History

The Queen's Hotel was situated on the south side of Queen Street next to the old Union bank building. In 1886, half an acre was sold to Ruth Coulter who had the hotel built on the property. It was stated that at Fair time Ruth would allow kids into the hotel and showed them the spread of ham, roast beef and pies.

At the back of the hotel there was a boarded in ice rink. There was also a tennis court to the side of the hotel and a wooden garage in the drive way. Alcoholic beverages were sold at the hotel followed by good times and company.

By the late 1930's the hotel was turned into apartments and eventually because of disrepair it was demolished.

The foundation of the building was bought by Willis Corrigan and was used in the last hand raised barn in the area. The lot now stands empty but at one time was listed as 13 Queen Street.

Sheila Trecartin picked up on two female spirits from two different eras in this location. The first spirit was from the 20th century. She was an older woman with grey hair and glasses and this spirit told Sheila she was a former banker in town. Sheila described her as nice person but stern with her job. She could be short tempered. She could also be strict and overpowering but once you got to know her and she liked you, she was wonderful. She dressed well and took pride in her job. This spirit stated, "Everyone in Cookstown knows me" and said she had a towel fetish. Sheila picked up a "J" name and said this woman died of cancer.

The other spirit Sheila picked up on was from the Victorian era. Sheila got the name of Tannis, but she did not know if that was a first or last name. This spirit was connected to the hotel and a coach house that was once at the back of the building. Amy was able to confirm through research that there was once a coach house at the back of the hotel.

Another spirit, who came from across the street, spoke to Sheila. Sheila told us that this was an older man with grey hair. He said he worked at the grocery store in 1919. He told Sheila he was the owner of the grocery store and had total pride in his business. He said he passed in the 1950's.

There were a couple of general/grocery stores in Cookstown at that time. We discovered that Henry Couse owned a grocery store in town from 1900 and carried on the business until his retirement in 1921. This grocery store was across the street from The Queen's Hotel. There was no way of knowing if this was the spirit who spoke to Sheila as he did not leave his name but Mr. Couse was a very prominent citizen of Cookstown at that time and was known to frequent the old hotel on delivery runs.

While the banker and the grocer were visiting spirits only, the ghost of the woman named Tannis does actually haunt this location. Why she haunts the location is a mystery. If you happen to witness her pale form in a Victorian dress as you walk down the street late at night, know you are not seeing things and you are not alone.

Image courtesy of the Cookstown Women's Institute, Tweedsmuir History

Grocery store owned by Henry Couse from 1900 - 1921

21 Queen Street
Thru The Grapevine

Amy is a member of the Cookstown Chamber of Commerce and was sitting in a meeting in this building in 2013 when she started to feel the presence of a spirit. This gave her the idea to do a book on the haunted buildings in Cookstown.

Thru the Grapevine gift shop is the current business at 21 Queen Street. Behind the store is a house which is still owned by the previous shop owner and council woman Lynn Dollin.

The original building was built in the mid 1800s. It was a house and then became a harness shop and then a shoe shop. Many owners later it became a flower shop in 1975. Lynn moved in and started her gift shop business in 1986.

The day we went to investigate Thru the Grapevine, we were greeted by Sue Sillers who works at the store. We immediately felt a presence upstairs where there were two open rooms. The spirit was friendly. As Sheila mounted the stairs, she received the impression of a baby bassinet at the top of the stairs. She said this was a memory. Sheila encountered the spirit of an older woman in her late 50's upstairs. She said this woman was a homemaker with an apron on and she was wiping her hands on the apron as if she had just done some baking. Sheila told us the spirit was very motherly, very protective. This was her home and Sheila sensed a child around her. Children were very important to her. The woman had rounded or puffy features and a warm face. She enjoyed sewing, crafts and quilt making. She told Sheila she liked that the place was open so that people could wander around and enjoy the space. She didn't like closed doors, secrets or people hiding things. She said when it was her house she had an herb garden in the back. She grew and used her own herbs. She explained that she knew the blacksmith and was close friends with him and that he still lingers as well. She said he was a respectful man who took pride in his work.

We realized that this store was once a harness shop and they would have dealt with the blacksmith. We put the timeline for this lady around the 1860's when the store was a harness shop owned by Charlie Hamilton. The Hamilton's lived above the shop and had a daughter, Hattie. We believe this spirit is Mrs. Hamilton. It is very likely she and her husband were good friends with the town blacksmith at that time and apparently she still enjoys his company today as well.

Blacksmith 3 King Street - 1887
Demolished in 1895

22 Queen Street
Timepiece

Walking up to this building today you will feel like you just stepped back in time. Ironically enough, the store is a clock repair shop called Timepiece.

The building was originally built in the late 1800s and was owned by Thomas Banting. He owned and operated a store called T.A.C. Banting Jeweller and Optician. In 1886, a telephone office was built within his store. In 1902, it was the official Bell telephone switch board for Cookstown and it stayed that way right up until 1960. While still having the switch board, it was also turned into a restaurant in 1970 and then a quilt shop in 1977.

The quilt shop was owned by Janette Kelly who was later murdered by her husband, an ex-Mountie, when they lived

Telephone Operators

in Toronto. Patrick Kelly was an undercover drug agent for the RCMP. They moved to Toronto and Janette was thrown off a balcony in 1981. Patrick collected the 250,000 insurance as he was having financial issues and then went and married his girlfriend. He was arrested in 1983.

After the Kelly's moved to Toronto, the building became a wicker shop and an art shop and in 1986 it became an antique store.

The Clock Store, established in 1994, is owned by Bogdan Lukaszek. Bogdan is a specialist in repairing and restoring antique clocks and fine watches. He told us he often felt spirits when he was alone working in the shop. Sheila Trecartin confirmed that there were many spirits in the store and they were connected or attached to the time pieces he was working on. Bogdan had a 1730 pocket watch he showed us and another clock in the store dated 1740. He had pieces from several time periods and countries, so we can only imagine how many spirits from different periods and places linger in the building.

Bogdan told us an interesting story. A woman customer brought in a clock to be repaired. She said it stopped at the time of her husband's death and would not start again. Bogdan worked on the clock in the store and found it was working fine. When she took the clock home, it stopped at the time her husband died and would not start again. She brought it back to the store. For a second time, Bogdan worked on the clock and it was working fine. When she took the clock home, it stopped again at the same time! She gave up after that. Bogdan told us this type of occurrence is not uncommon and has happened to him before.

Sheila picked up on two spirits who were personally connected to Bogdan. The first was a woman spirit who would come around at night and watch as Bogdan repaired or worked on time pieces. That woman identified herself as his wife's aunt. The second spirit was Bogdan's own grandfather who also liked to come and watch his grandson work on the clocks as well.

Sheila then picked up a male spirit. She said he worked on men's clothing and was a tailor. He said he owned his own building and would give business to a shoemaker. He complained of lower back problems.

While doing research on the building, Amy found out it was never used as a clothing store and then she made a startling discovery. There was once a building beside the Clock Store called "Eby & Co. Merchant Tailors" established in 1899. Mr. Eby stayed in business until 1927 when the store changed hands. This building burned down in 1939 taking the Mansion Hotel with it. We realized that Sheila was picking up on the tailor from next door, Mr. W.J. Eby. With his building destroyed by fire, it is very possible he occupied the building next door.

Mr. Eby talked about the shoemaker he gave business too. Across the street from his tailor store was a shoe shop with a shoemaker at that time. William Montgomery bought his store in 1872 and made and sold shoes until he passed in 1943. That building is now Thru the Grapevine at 21 Queen Street.

Image courtesy of the Cookstown Women's Institute, Tweedsmuir History

Mr. Eby's Store

71 Queen Street
Joan's Story

Joan McLean is 94 years old and is considered the town historian. She wrote a book called, "Glimpses of Cookstown 1825-1991". This historic document of the buildings in the town and the people who occupied them has been an invaluable source for our research. Joan loves to do paintings of the historic buildings in Cookstown as well. Coincidentally, her family came from Cookstown, Ireland in 1825 and started the United Church in town. Her great, great aunt, Mary Ann Kidd, was the wife of Mr. Thomas Cooke, the town founder.

Joan had heard of Sheila Trecartin and called her to get help regarding the spirits in her home. She lives at 71 Queen Street. The property was the site of a saw mill and gristmill and in 1929 the local creamery was located there until 1951. The Department of Highways had used the property when the road along Hwy 89 was raised and drainage ditches were built following Hurricane Hazel in 1958. The current home was built in 1972 and Joan said her family has been the sole occupant of it.

Image courtesy of the Cookstown Women's Institute, Tweedsmuir History

Gristmill

Sheila revealed the following about her home:

"There is a bit of a through way in her home. It is a place where spirits pass through.

There is an older man in the back bedroom that seems to have taken up residence there. There are many that walk through but do not stay. Some of what she is going through are the ghosts and other layers are her fears. As we get closer to passing sometimes our awareness of spirit heightens. This doesn't mean she will pass soon, it just means that her body is recognizing the transition is occurring and reacting to it by slowly opening up the perceptions of the other side. It is a slow gentle transition and some get to experience this while others have more of a quick transition experience. She should not fear. The ghosts that are around her are not harmful, just playful or mischievous. The air thing does bother me. It is stagnant in there with heavy old energies. It needs to be lifted and cleared. First the fear has to be extinguished then the energy cleared."

We discovered the man in the back bedroom was Joan's husband who had passed on. He liked to hang out in his old home and bedroom and visit his wife. Joan didn't appreciate the "mischievous or playful" antics of the ghosts who moved things on her. She complained of papers taken out of her filing cabinets. She said tea, coffee, cheese, ice cream, cookies and candy went missing or was moved. Lipsticks were taken out of her vanity and spatulas were taken out of the cupboard.

Joan told us she has heard footsteps at night and has seen two ladies in her living room by the television, a gentleman in the house and even a small Japanese child. Her biggest complaint was the stagnant air. She said she had to open windows and keep fans blowing to clear it.

Joan has no intention of moving and will continue to live with the spirits but will ask them to stop moving things on her in future.

King Street
Thomas Cooke's Manor

Image courtesy of the Cookstown Women's Institute, Tweedsmuir History

If you travel down the south side of Highway 27 almost out of town you will see a house like no other in Cookstown. It was, in its time, a grand estate.

The first house on the property was built in 1839 by Thomas Cooke and was called Ravenscraig. However, it wasn't as grand as the place you see today. In 1868, Ravenscraig was completed as a huge manor at a cost of $50,000. In

1872, it was remodeled for gas lighting and other grand improvements. It boasted 11 bedrooms, a powder room, wood panels, an orchestra pit and the biggest ballroom north of Toronto. It was said the Cooke family would host 30 parties in one season.

In 1907, a veterinarian bought the house and ended up severing off the land around the estate. In 1956 it was sold again and then made into 6 apartments. The name changed to Hindle Manor. Cookstown residents thought they were crazy for doing such a thing to the beautiful grand house but the apartments are still rented out to this day.

We drove down Hwy 27 on a sunny but chilly morning with medium Sheila Trecartin. We parked along the road by the old manor and almost immediately Sheila made contact with Mr. Thomas Cooke himself, who was the founder of the town, although she did not realize who she was talking to at the time. Mr. Cooke came right up to the car window and started to talk to Sheila.

Sheila described an older serious gentleman with a prominent high profile position. He said he was under a lot of pressure to make the right choices and decisions where the town was concerned. He spent most of his time between his family and work. He was often sought after for guidance and had to be stern, mean and abrupt at times but he stated that he didn't like to be like that. He said he spent a good deal of time overseeing land registries and writing and signing documents. People made a lot of demands on his time and he tried to remain courteous and respectful. He told Sheila he loved his children and he loved birds but he said he didn't love his wife. He said it was a marriage of convenience. Sheila saw six children laughing and playing with a nanny.

Later on, Amy discovered that Mr. Cooke did have 6 children; James, Christopher, Thomas, George, Sarah and Mary Ann when she was researching his biography. Amy also discovered that Mr. Cooke's marriage to Mary Ann Kidd was not a happy one and his wife liked to spend his money. She discovered Mr. Cooke registered lots for sale at the Registry office in Barrie under the name "Cookes Town". He died in 1875.

Mr. Cooke told Sheila that the stables were once behind and to the right of the manor and he had the best well in town. He said there were more trees surrounding the property when he lived there. He talked about his carriage with black horses and said many parties were held at the house. He explained that 1937 was an important year for the house but didn't say in what way. Unfortunately, we were not able to find out with our historical research when happened in 1937.

Mr. Cooke said he wanted to build a beautiful house for stature and brought in prestigious items and furniture from Europe. He spoke of a wooden credenza/cabinet brought from Italy with intricate woodwork and he said that he liked the two tone wood.

He spoke of a wedding held on the property with a white tent erected for the big event with games and contests being held in the field. He went on to describe a horse pull.

Mr. Cooke explained that the house once had a rounded driveway. He said a stone mason died while working on the house and he thought at the time that would bring bad luck. He said he was superstitious and had the house blessed and placed a cross in the home. He described himself as a religious man who prayed a lot. He also said he was never a slim man and he loved food and drink.

He talked about the area being a trading place for spices and said the town doctor was his good friend, advisor and confidant. He also talked about Upper Canada and an agreement that had passed in the early 1800's about the community. His only regret was that his original vision for the town had not been followed. He still visits his home from time to time and is impressed that the structure has held up well and he is glad it is still utilized. He stated he only had what he did because of his father and he owed everything to him.

As we were leaving, he courteously thanked Sheila for listening to him and continued his walk along Hwy. 27.

18 King St. S
Amy's Story

1854 is the earliest entry at the registry office for this property, when Thomas Cooke sold a half acre to William Sutherland.

In March 1856, Sutherland sold the land to Thomas R. Ferguson for 415 pounds and a house constructed by John Ross was later built on the property. In 1871, a man named McMaster sold the property and house to Isaac Ferguson.

Issac Ferguson was the father of Emily Murphy. Amy explained that this home may have been Emily Murphy's childhood home. According to the book, "Memories of Cookstown" written by the Innisfil Historical Society, Emily served as Canada's first female Police Magistrate in the British Empire and a judge in the Alberta Juvenile Court.

Murphy was part of the Famous Five, who took the issue of women's rights to the highest courts in Canada and England, securing their status as legal persons in 1929.

The house burned down sometime between 1871 and 1889 and was rebuilt by Mr. Ferguson. It had a large stable behind the house. The house was bought and sold to a few families over the years. In 1968, Chester and Irma Adams bought the house and it was eventually owned by one of their children making them the longest family to stay on the property. Chester liked to repair antique cars in the old stable. When Amy and her family looked at the house in 2011, they just knew they were home.

The first thing Sheila sensed as she walked towards the house was a Victorian woman in her 30's. She was described as a brunette with a bonnet and she wore granny boots. She liked to sit in a rocker on the front porch. Sheila discovered from the spirit that she was left a childless widow when her husband died suddenly. Sheila described her as lonely, depressed and detached from life. After her husband died, she lived with her husband's parents, who occupied the downstairs of the home while she lived upstairs. She still occupies the upstairs of the house. She complained to Sheila that she was upset with the floor plan of the current home. The stairs were on the wrong side and it used to be more open, she said. We realized she lived in the original home before it burned down and was rebuilt.

This spirit said there were a lot of apple orchards around

her when she lived in the home and she loved to make apple pies. Sheila picked up a date of 1872. She said something serious happened then. We felt she was giving us the year when the fire burned the house down.

Going up the stairs, Sheila felt a strong vortex at the top landing. When we entered the bedroom to the right of the stairs, we were overcome with an anxious energy. This was from the woman on the porch. Sheila explained to us that she was in despair after the sudden death of her husband and committed suicide by taking a white powder. Arsenic or some kind of rodent poison came to mind. Sheila said this woman was content staying upstairs and liked to watch over Amy's children and didn't want to go to the other side. Amy picked up the name Margaret and felt that was possibly the spirit's name. At first, we thought Margaret may have been married to one of Mr. Ferguson's sons but upon research Amy found out that all his sons lived until the 1920's. We realized that Margaret was tied to one of the earlier families who once owned the land and building.

In Amy's bedroom, Sheila picked up another spirit who liked to come and visit often. Sheila discovered it was the grandmother of either Amy or her husband Brent.

Downstairs in the front parlour, Sheila sensed there was once a coffin in the front window. Amy confirmed that she often had that feeling. In Victorian times, the coffin of a deceased loved one was often placed in the front parlour of the home. Sheila explained that the front parlour of this home was frequently used for wakes even by the neighbours.

Sheila further sensed that the house sat on a Ley line with river energy flowing through the basement. She also picked up that it was once farm land with cows and sheep. When Amy's husband Brent was doing renovation work, he came across ashes and animal bones in the basement.

In the kitchen at the back of the house, Sheila saw another spirit. She described him as 6 feet tall with grey hair and green overalls. She said he was a happy soul and a former owner in the 1960's who was very proud of his home, especially his workshop in the backyard. That workshop is still standing.

This was not the first time Amy had heard that description of the spirit. Months before, she had a visit from a friend, Trish Hubel. Her friend also had psychic abilities and told Amy that there was a happy man in the kitchen wearing green overalls. Another medium once gave Amy the name "Chester".

Amy said when she first moved into the home, she was in bed half asleep when a man of this description poked his head in the door. Amy, in a drowsy state said to him, "I'm sorry but we live here now". The spirit said, "Okay" and with that disappeared and Amy fell asleep. On another occasion after deciding to help write this book, Amy was tucked into bed when she happened to open her eyes and saw this same man look back at her by her night table and then he disappeared. She described him as an older gentleman with a square face. Amy said it was quite odd because it was dark and she cannot see without her glasses but she described him as a transparent figure with white outlines. Amy said that after seeing that she closed her eyes and did not want to open them again until morning.

Amy knows that Chester Adams, the former resident of 18 King St. South, meant her no harm. She admits that she did want to see a ghost and Chester may have allowed that reality to happen. Amy said she often sensed this happy spirit in the kitchen enjoying the social times they frequently had with family and friends.

Amy is comfortable with both Chester and Margaret in her house. She considers them part of the family and treats them both with the same love and respect they show her family.

Image courtesy of the Cookstown Women's Institute, Tweedsmuir History

1 Hamilton St.
South Simcoe Theatre

One of the most haunted buildings in Cookstown is the South Simcoe Theatre on Hamilton Street. The theatre has been a landmark in the town since 1867, the year of Confederation. Over the years, the building has been used as a temperance hall and meeting hall funded by the Lodge of the Good Templars. It was used as a Presbyterian church in 1869 and it was declared a town hall in 1905. In 1983, it became the South Simcoe Theatre.

The theatre has been investigated by the Haunted Barrie Meetup group on a number of occasions. The following appeared in the Innisfil Scope on August 28, 2013 in the article, "The Ghosts of Simcoe County": Actors, actresses, stagehands and paranormal investigators have witnessed poltergeist activity, heard voices and have seen apparitions over the many years the theatre has been open. During an investigation of the Haunted Barrie Meetup Group, they were able to capture several EVP's which contained quite clear disembodied voices and sounds. They picked up whispering in the sound booth area and there was also physical contact reported by two seasoned investigators. On audio, they heard a child giggling and whistling. A recorder in the basement picked up piano music which no one heard in the building until they listened to the recording the next day. Two investigators were in the sound booth when they both saw a shadow figure walk across the stage. Another member of the group saw a female shadow figure on the back stairs behind the stage. While an investigator was sitting in the theatre audience seats with a psychic, she felt something or someone walk around her. She then felt a touch on her shoulder and nearly jumped out of her chair

Image courtesy of the Cookstown Women's Institute, Tweedsmuir History

when she felt a hand put pressure on her knee. The psychic sitting beside her was able to confirm a male energy, "He wants you to pay attention to him and confirm for everyone he is right there".

Sandy Bishop and Kathy Simpson have been with the theatre for many years. Sandy joined in 1995 and Kathy joined in 2001. They both do everything and anything for the theatre which is greatly supported by the town of Innisfil. Kathy and Sandy explained that they are both sensitive to the spirit world and have great respect for the spirits who frequent the theatre. They explained that the theatre has a portal in it and that allows the spirits to freely come and go. "Spirits don't linger here for long but the activity is constant", Kathy said.

Sandy explained that the show itself always draws a certain type of spirit. A comedy will often draw a happy crowd whereas a tragedy will draw a sad crowd. The energy of the play attracts the same energy of spirit. Kathy remembered when they were doing a comedy play about a dead man called, "Lucky Stiff", the spirits were not happy with the play at all. They found the topic disrespectful and did everything in their power to disrupt the show. Lights would be turned on and off, objects would be knocked off tables, the lighting board and sound board were played with and settings were constantly changed.

A spirit once showed up to be cast in a play. The director had picked his cast and had an equal number of actresses and actors and divided them into two specific groups. When he did a recount, an actor was missing, "Where did the gentleman go who was standing right here?" he asked the group. They were all surprised and one of the actors said there was never anyone standing beside him.

One time when an actress forgot her line, a spirit whispered the words in her ear. When she turned to thank the person, no one was there. Spirits also accompanied a singer in a play. When she stopped singing, the ghostly voices carried on with the song.

There have been reports of the hand dryer in the bathroom going on and off by itself, reports of orbs, many people feel their hair being played with, many people have heard thumps going up and down the stairs and the sounds of hammering and banging behind the curtain when no one was there.

When asked about specific spirits they have known in the past, Kathy and Sandy mentioned a few. They talked about the tragic spirit of a black farm hand from the 1800's who lingered in the upper level of the theatre. He was caught having a relationship with the farmer's daughter. The father discovered them and was so enraged he had the farm hand hung in his barn.

They also talked about an Irish family who stayed in the theatre. There was the father, mother and their little mischievous daughter who liked to play with the hand dryer and tell people to "ssshhhh" when they were talking too loudly.

Both Sandy and Kathy spoke of Gerrard, a sure of himself, cocky spirit who liked to hang out in the sound booth. "He set himself up as boss of the spirit world in the theatre", they explained. "He enjoyed the theatre and he didn't like people coming in to mess with the spirits at all." A while ago Gerrard asked a medium to release him. The medium sent him to the light. Gerrard is at peace now and no longer frequents the sound booth or the building.

Finally, the ladies talked about "the dark slug". This was a negative black blob of energy that appeared at a time when there was a lot of conflicts during a transition period with the theatre. They explained there was a lot of negative feelings and things going on at the time and said the blob was feeding off of this negative energy. Sandy remembers running into "the dark slug" when she was coming down the stairs and said it just exuded a horrible nasty energy. Thankfully, it is long gone.

Kathy and Sandy welcome you to the theatre but ask that you always show respect to the spirits in the building.

On the day of the investigation, Amy arrived early and toured the building first. When Cate arrived, Amy took her to the main theatre and asked her to tell her what she felt. When Cate walked up on the stage, she felt a force literally pull her to the right hand side of the stage behind the curtain area. Amy said the exact same thing happened to her. Amy and Cate both felt a very strong spirit just waiting off in the wings behind the curtain. Amy and Cate were also drawn to the dressing room below the area downstairs.

In April, Amy went to see the play "Dracula" put on by the theatre. Right before the play started she experienced a rush of pressure around her and felt like she was being suffocated. After the play started the feeling went away. At intermission, as everyone went down the stairs, she became very dizzy. She said she felt like the spirits were leaving with everyone else.

On the day medium Sheila Trecatin came to do an investigation of the building, she said she felt head pain and pressure when we pulled up to the front of the theatre. She confirmed that there was a portal or thorough way in the building in the back right hand corner. This explained why Amy and Cate were pulled in that direction during their earlier investigation. The stage area they were drawn to and the dressing room downstairs are located in the back right hand corner of the building. When Amy went to see the play Dracula she was also seated at the front right of the stage nearest the portal. As the play started, she felt all the spirits rushing in.

Sheila picked up 5 spirits in the building the day of her investigation. The first spirit was an older, solemn woman. She was a secretary and took care of the books, accounts and records when the building was a town hall. She also picked up the spirit of a male dentist who died of a heart attack in the building when it was a town hall.

Sheila picked up two spirits who were attached to the theatre itself. The first spirit was a heavy set woman who liked to sing. She was in the curtain area where Amy and Cate were originally drawn. This woman spirit told Sheila she was very proud of the theatre and that the theatre was her life. We have to wonder if this is the same spirit who carried on singing after the actress had finished her song. We also have to wonder if this is the spirit who whispered the line to the actress who forgot it. This could also be the same woman spirit that the Haunted Barrie Meetup group saw on the back stairs and the shadow figure that crossed the stage when they were doing their investigation.

Sheila also picked up on a male spirit attached to the theatre. He was sitting in one of the theatre audience seats. Sheila described him as a nice man who was clean cut. He showed her a picture of the Headless Horseman. Sheila had no idea why. Either this was a play that the theatre put on at one time or it may be a play he wants to see. We have to wonder if this is the male spirit who put his hand on the shoulder and knee of the investigator with the Haunted Barrie Meetup group while she was sitting in the audience because he wanted attention and to be noticed. We also have to wonder if this male spirit was the missing actor who once turned up to be cast in a play and then disappeared.

Finally, Sheila picked up a shy, reserved 17 or 18 year old girl. She died of small pox in the late 1800's. She said her father was a prominent businessman in town. Her father owned the building when it was run by the Good Templars and he spent a lot of time in the building. She said she lived close by with her father and she came to the building frequently when he was working there. She didn't seem to want to leave and move on. She has been haunting the place for a long time.

If you visit the theatre, please enjoy the show but don't be surprised if that empty seat beside you is already taken by someone not of this world.

18 Church St.
The Curling Club

We had received a tip that the Curling Club which was originally built as a Men's Club in 1956 was haunted. Cate went to the club and found two gentlemen at the bar. She approached them and introduced herself and told them we were writing a ghost book on Cookstown and asked if they would be interested in being investigated for spirits. It turned out that the two gentlemen were the President and Vice President of the Club. Fabio, the President, immediately said yes and Keith, the VP, turned to Fabio and exclaimed, "I knew there were ghosts here! See I told you!"

We were later contacted by Leo, the Secretary-Treasurer at the Club, and we set up an appointment on a Saturday morning to begin the investigation. While we waited for

Leo, we ended up chatting with Linda who was the cleaner for the building. She told us she felt comfortable working at the club but she did feel there was a spirit in the Ladies Lounge downstairs. She said it always felt a little bit depressing in that room. Jill who was tending bar at the time told us the creepiest place in the club was the room below the bar. She said she didn't like to go down there at all.

After that, Leo showed up to talk to us about his experiences and to give us a tour of the Club. Leo told us he was in the bar area one night by himself. Everyone had left and he was alone in the building when he thought he saw a shadow or figure move out of the corner of his eye. He then heard something move from the cooler to the kitchen. When he looked back towards the kitchen the large, heavy clear plastic flaps in the doorway were swinging back and forth. He said he actually called Vern, a volunteer who was the last to leave the club, to see if he locked up before he left

Image courtesy of the Cookstown Women's Institute, Tweedsmuir History

Curling Club before addition.

because he was not sure if someone was in the building or not. Vern said he locked up everything and even checked the door. Leo said he literally felt the hair on the back of his neck go up. He said it was just an odd moment and he couldn't explain what he saw or heard.

When Leo took us back to the kitchen area, we couldn't sense anything, but as he led us down the stairs by the cooler, Cate stopped and blurted out, "there is someone here on the stairs". We kept going downstairs to the room below the bar. This room was actually the old bar that was used in the club in the 1950's. We both felt a strong presence in this room. Cate was expecting a creepy atmosphere after hearing from Jill, but to her surprise, she felt the spirit of a really fun character and actually started laughing out loud.

After that, Leo took us to the Ladies lounge. Amy went to one side of the lounge and said she felt nothing there. Cate was in the older section of the lounge with the lockers and did feel the spirit of a woman and described her as "shy".

We asked Leo if we could arrange another day to come back to the Club and if we could bring Sheila Trecartin with us as Sheila was very open to spirit and could confirm if there were ghosts in the building. Leo said yes and we arranged for Sheila to come with us on another weekend. As with every building we investigate, we never let Sheila know where we are going or what we had discovered.

Leo took Sheila on the same tour of the building. To our surprise, she stopped on the same part of the stairs that Cate did and said, "There is a man here by the cooler." The spirit told Sheila that the cooler was not always there. Leo confirmed that the cooler was put in in the mid 1980's. Sheila picked up that this man had a funny eye, bad knees and a liver problem from drinking. She said he did odd jobs and would fix things. She also picked up that he had a dog. She got a collie cross and said the dog was brown and black and was connected to the man. She said he still walked the property a lot with his dog. Sheila stated that he was not stuck but he chose to be the guardian of the club. It meant a lot to him and he was a shareholder. Sheila said if he didn't like someone he would bug them and was gruff. He said he didn't mind Leo and he didn't bother him. Sheila picked up a "B" name and said he didn't want women to join the club.

Right away, Leo said it sounded like Bill Marling. He explained that this was once a club for men only and when they debated allowing women, Bill did not want that to happen. Leo said Bill was adamantly opposed to women joining and he didn't want the club to change. Leo confirmed that he drank and would sometimes wear a patch over his one bad eye. Leo pointed out that he lived across the parking lot and was a guardian for the club. The house was no longer there and was torn down a while ago. Leo said Bill died at the age of 82. Sheila said that Bill wanted a picture of himself put up in the old men's room.

After that, Leo escorted Sheila down to the old bar room downstairs. He didn't tell her what the room was used for. Sheila picked up men playing "games and cards and drinking". She picked up several people and said, "There were some playboys down here". She picked up that some women came down here to be with some of the men. That surprised Leo since it was a men's club only but he did get a confirmation later on from another board member who said that did happen in the 70's and 80's. Sheila picked up the old bartender, Sandy Thompson, and described him as a "jovial, fun, joking extrovert with light hair". This had to be the spirit who made Cate laugh.

The old bar area downstairs.

When we went back upstairs, Sheila picked up on a "Harry Ross" whom she described as a jack of all trades jokester who would come and go from the club. Leo was nodding his head in agreement. He knew of Harry and his son Brian and he even pointed out Harry's picture on the wall. Harry said he liked Leo a lot and he was always welcome in the family. When Leo told Sheila about his experience with the moving flaps by the kitchen, she said that was Harry. He had a real comical side but didn't mean to scare Leo.

When Leo took Sheila into the ice rink, she felt the residual energy of laughter and fun. Spirit also told her that the roof at the back of the rink required some repairs.

The final stop on the tour was the Ladies Lounge and Locker Room. The room has two sections separated by a door. Sheila said the energy stopped at the door. Leo explained that the one side of the room was a newer section that was added on recently. This would explain why Amy felt nothing when she was exploring that side. Sheila did pick up on a woman spirit on the locker side of the lounge. This was the same woman Cate picked up on. Cate told Sheila she thought the spirit was "shy". Sheila said she was not shy but quiet. She said she learned not to speak unless she had something to say. Sheila described the woman as being in her late 50's to early 60's. She had brown hair and glasses and was wearing a cream and red sweater and was really nice. She was a heavier woman with bigger hips. She wasn't stuck and would come and go. She said she really liked it at the club and her husband passed a little earlier then she did. Apparently, they both came to the club a lot.

It was certainly wonderful to get confirmation from Leo that everything Sheila was saying was accurate and it was really helpful that he actually knew most of the spirits when they were living on this side of the veil.

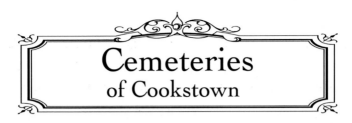

Cemeteries
of Cookstown

The cemetery on Church Street was on land that was originally owned by the Ferguson family and this land was given to the town by the family. This is the same family who built and lived in Amy's current home on King Street.

The cemetery is divided into 3 sections; those who died and were buried in the 1800's to 1900 are in one section. Those who died and were buried between 1900 and 2000 are in another section and the third section is for those who died and were buried from 2000 on. There is a marker in the cemetery dated 1754 or 1757 but most burials happened after the 1800's.

When we drove Sheila to the site, she stated there were a

lot of spirits in the cemetery. She explained that they love to meet their loved ones who come to visit their graves and she told us this was common in cemeteries. Sheila said this cemetery was really busy with spirits at Christmas time.

Sheila made connection with two spirits when we were at the site. The first was an older woman with glasses, brown hair with a heavier build. She told Sheila she was a secretary in the town between the 1940's and 1960's. This spirit was just visiting that day.

The other spirit was a ghost girl. This little girl was about nine or ten years old with blonde braided hair. Sheila said she had on a pretty dress with ruffles and black buckled shoes. Sheila stated she had been around for many years. The little girl told Sheila she died suddenly and her family

didn't come to visit her grave anymore. When Sheila asked her why she was still at the cemetery, she shrugged and told Sheila she just liked to hang out there and play.

We are happy to report that Sheila successfully crossed this little girl over to the other side.

Former Cookstown resident Wesley Frigault shared the following story and photos of the cemetery along highway 27:

Wesley Frigault's Photo of an orb over a tombstone.

"I've been here on a few occasions and have had some crazy stuff happen. There is one tombstone that is off by itself and the writing is facing the wrong way. One night a good friend and I were here taking pictures with our digital cameras. I went around to the front of the stone and turned on my camera and it died just as my flashlight went out too. As soon as I came back out to meet my friend, I tried to turn on my camera and it turned on without a problem. Then I noticed that I had 3 pictures taken in front of the stone and the time was the same in all 3 pictures. I have no way to prove that my story is true but I swear to you I did not take these pictures and the camera was not on."

We have seen many orbs on ghost photos. Some can be explained as natural phenomenon like rain or dust particles or something on or in the camera, while others simply cannot be explained and are viewed as supernatural.

Paranormal author Cynthia Silk divides orbs into 3 main categories:

1. Spirit orbs typically represent the energies of people who once lived a life here. Spirit energies are most commonly found in cemeteries, sites where multiple deaths took place or where crimes were committed, natural disaster sites and abandoned buildings such as prisons, psychiatric hospitals or former POW camps. Spirit orbs are usually white or off white in color.

2. Angel orbs represent the presence of Angels and they can be found anywhere there is life. Angel orbs however are far more complex than spirit orbs because they can also contain messages, symbols or pictures. Angel orbs are seen

in many colors – white, blue, green and purple are among the most significant.

3. Nature orbs are a common phenomenon that are often mistaken for spirit or angel orbs. These particular types of orbs are produced by nature and are a direct result of many of its elements. The most common orbs produced by nature occur during rain showers, snow storms or extreme weather conditions such as hurricanes. These orbs are typically gray in color when captured on film. Nature orbs can also be found where sunlight is prevalent. Sunlight orbs are among the most beautiful because of their colorful composition and can be easily captured on film.

We have a feeling that the young man who died at the age of 32 in 1908 was trying to get Wesley's attention when he was around his tombstone. Spirits are energy and they can drain the energy from the batteries of cameras and flashlights and other devices. This is a common occurrence for ghost hunters or people who come into contact with a spirit. The mystery lies in the fact that the camera went dead, according to Wesley, when the three photos were taken at the same time.

19 Elizabeth St.
The Old Hospital

The old hospital used in the last century in Cookstown is now a private residence. The land was bought in 1861 and a house was built on it and lived in by a few families until 1920 when it was turned into a hospital. The dining room was used as the operating room. The doctor would work by lantern light while operating on a patient.

In 1945, the hospital was sold as a private home and was purchased by a family who had 4 children. Their father was later killed in a train accident. The home changed owners a few more times after that.

The current owners of the blue home at 19 Elizabeth Street (at the corner of East John Street) are Doug and Mardi

Black. Doug explained that his own mother was operated on at Stevenson Memorial Hospital in Alliston in 1930. Her appendix had erupted when she was nine years old. This was considered a death sentence at that time unless measures were taken quickly. Doug Black explained that the old doctor at the time opened up his mother and did his best to clean out the mess of the eruption. He was not too careful putting all of her insides back in, because she would probably die anyway. Not many survived such incidences in the 1930's. Somehow, she survived the surgery and recovered. She remained frail and anemic for many years.

After his mother got married, she discovered that she could not have children. During a routine surgery, in the 1950's, another doctor opened up his mother only to see the mess the old doctor had made. The doctor said things were not where they were supposed to be inside her body. The doctor fixed the mistakes. Her metabolism improved immensely. It was clear that all of the misplacements had disrupted her life completely, but she had lived against all odds. After this surgery, Doug's mother got pregnant and gave birth to him.

Doug Black said they moved back to Cookstown when he was older to look after his elderly mother. They purchased the blue home at 19 Elizabeth Street unaware that is was the old hospital in Cookstown. He bought it because it had a downstairs bedroom which would suit his mother who found it difficult to climb stairs. When his mother came to the home, she could sense something was very wrong with the place. She felt scared and uneasy in the building

Doug only found out, after his mother's death, that this was the hospital where she would have come for follow-up visits after her horrible experience. Now it all made sense. Her discomfort derived from horrible subconscious memories combined with the uneasiness she felt which came from the fact that there were also spirits in the building.

Doug described a woman spirit who liked to bake in the kitchen late at night. He would often wake up to the smell of cookies, bread and other baked goods in the early hours of the morning. Doug also explained that there was a ghost girl in the house who repeatedly turned the bathroom lights on and off and turned the TV off randomly. The house also came with an angry, mean spirited man who liked to push people down the stairs. Doug had been pushed many times by this ghost. It became so bad Doug had to have the home exorcised twice to get rid of him.

You have to wonder if these spirits died in the old hospital and ended up staying around. Perhaps, like Doug's mother, they were also victims of the old doctor's careless surgery, only perhaps these patients weren't as lucky as his mother.

As a final note, Doug explained that the old doctor is said to still haunt his old home at the other end of Elizabeth Street in Cookstown.

When we took medium Sheila Trecartin to investigate the old hospital, she picked up on 4 spirits. She didn't know

Doug or Mardi Black or what they had been through in the house and she didn't know that this building was once a hospital. We parked on the road beside the house and right away Sheila picked up the spirit of a little girl with a yellow dress and black hair. After that, Cate let Sheila know that Doug did say there was a young girl in the house who played with the bathroom lights and TV.

Next, Sheila picked up on a woman spirit. Sheila said she sits in a front room on the right side of the house. Sheila said this woman was a nurse and she sits in a little room that was once a treatment room. At that point, Cate told Sheila that this house was a former hospital.

After that, Sheila picked up on another woman spirit. Cate was shocked when she said, "this lady hangs out in the kitchen and likes baking." She then told Sheila that Doug frequently woke up to the smells of baking from the kitchen in the middle of the night.

Finally, Sheila picked up on the spirit of a scared little boy who was playing with toy cars in an upstairs room of the house, possibly the attic. She picked up the name of Daniel and she said he felt lost and felt abandoned. Sheila said Daniel doesn't move from this space. He was told to hide here. Sheila could not understand what he was told to hide from. Sheila picked up that Daniel's mother was Rose. She called in Rose and asked her to take Daniel to the light. We are happy to report that Daniel is no longer in the house and has gone to his heavenly home with his mother.

Sheila saw a crawl space with a dirt floor downstairs in the basement and said they use to put the dead people in there. These were the patients who died in the hospital.

Cate told Sheila that Doug had the home exorcised twice to get rid of an angry and mean spirit who was pushing him and others down the stairs. Sheila identified this spirit as a male psychiatric patient who used to be strapped down. She confirmed that the exorcism worked and he was gone from the house.

As Cate and Sheila drove away from the old hospital, a spirit named Margaret from East John Street approached the car while they were at a stop sign waiting to turn left. Margaret told Sheila she knew a lot about the history of Cookstown and wanted to be in our book! We have kept our promise to Margaret and we certainly hope she can rest in peace now!

5108 Hwy 27
Cookstown Antique Market

The Cookstown Antique Market is located just north of Hwy 89 on the west side of Hwy 27, beside the Cookstown public school. The 6,000 square foot century old barn is the home of 35 antique dealers. The Cookstown Antique Market is truly a collector's haven with a fine collection of vintage memorabilia. As soon as you walk into the Antique Market in Cookstown you become overwhelmed by the residual energy coming from the antiques themselves.

Gerry and Sally Robinson are the owners and operators of the Cookstown Antique Market. The home was built around 1905 by a Mr. Glass, a local builder. In the spring of 1993, the barn, which was originally constructed in 1875, was purchased and moved from a farm in Springwater Township with the help of Mr. Rudy Weiderer, a post and beam specialist from Essa Township. One year later, Mr. Weiderer suffered a heart attack and sadly passed away at the young age of forty two. He engraved his name in a beam in the upstairs of the barn.

Gerry and Sally feel that a few spirits came with the building. "Objects fall off the shelves when no one is around. Cups are broken fairly often. Our two employees, Debbie and Lori, frequently hear from customers that they sense presences in the building or see shadows moving. There is someone here." Even the family dog has been known to jump back from certain spots including the office in the barn.

Upon investigation, we were drawn, or even pulled towards the entrance by the stairs. We were also overwhelmed by a strong energy coming from the old clocks and radios on the second floor of the barn.

When we brought medium Sheila Trecartin with us to do an investigation of the area, she was also drawn to the entrance by the stairs. We thought this was a possible portal for spirits but Sheila said there was water under the ground in that area. We all acted like human dowsers and were pulled right to the spot.

Sheila picked up 3 spirits in the barn. The first spirit was that of a man from the early 1800's. The spirit told Sheila the coach house was in front of the barn. This is where

Gerry's office is located. This was a man from a wealthy family who had high end horses. This spirit said he liked to ride, had a lot of money and didn't work very hard. He was the wealthy, taken care of son in the family. The word spoiled came to mind. Sheila told us he was acting like a child, very moody and possessive and very materialistic. He didn't want to give up his space and the coach house was where he spent a great deal of his time when he was alive. He does not want to share the coach house and he is not happy people are still using his space since he still owns it in his mind. This man told Sheila when he was 30, he fell off his horse, hit his head and neck and died instantly. Sheila called him mischievous and said he likes to stir the pot. He wants to be acknowledged. Sheila said when cups are broken or objects fall off the shelves, it is his spirit doing it.

The second spirit Sheila picked up was another male. This was a farmhand in the barn who worked for the parents of the spoiled son. Sheila described him as round, burly and quiet. She said he had hip problems and walked with a limp. He died when he was an older man. Sheila said when he brushes by people in the barn they often feel a wind or breeze. Sheila also told us that there was the spirit of a happy little black dog in the barn as well. Cate picked up the names Jonathan and Robert and felt the names may have been connected to the two male spirits in the barn.

The dog and the farmhand do not cause any problems in the barn. However, Jonathan or Robert, the wealthy son, is restless and wants attention. Acknowledging this spirit might just be the trick in getting him to settle down and stop breaking cups, dishes and other fragile items.

Entrance of the barn where we were drawn to.

18 King St. N
Ghost Dog

We were contacted by the owners who moved into this 45 year old home 2 years ago. They said they often found puddles of water in different rooms of the house and there was no logical explanation for it. They found puddles of water in the kitchen, an upstairs bedroom, the laundry room downstairs and the recreation room downstairs. The puddles would appear and disappear again. They said the toilet would sometimes flush by itself and they often heard what sounded like footsteps in the hallway late at night when they were in bed.

While standing in the area where the mysterious puddles appeared, Cate got the sense of an animal, a dog to be precise. Amy confirmed that the land around the house was once swampy which would explain the puddles. Cate left the home with the distinct impression that what was haunting the home was not a person but an animal and it was friendly. It was just trying to get attention that it was there by leaving puddles and walking in the hall and even playing with the toilet handle.

The owner took us back to the garage behind their house. He said he often felt uneasy working in the garage area and at times has felt the need to grab a steel bar or something for self-protection. He said he felt someone watching him and it made him feel uneasy. We both picked up an angry or agitated male presence in the garage. We didn't feel this spirit was attached to the house or the garage but was connected to the land around him.

We told the owner to protect himself with white light when he worked in the garage but he had nothing to fear from his house.

When we wrote to Sheila about the house, she had this to say:

Hi Ladies,
Thanks for the update. I have been in that house before. A light haired lady babysat my son for a bit that lived in that house. They had a black dog. I am sure he has passed now. That dog was extremely protective of the property and would sit for hours outside on the steps and lawn guarding the house. I never felt anything negative when I was in the

house. I never went near the garage.

Sheila Trecartin

animal communicator & holistic therapist

We later took Sheila over to the house to see what she could pick up on. This is one time where Sheila was aware of the story because we did write to her about the house after our investigation to see if it was possible if an animal could haunt a building. Sheila did confirm that it was the spirit of the dog inside the house.

We then went to the garage area where the owner felt disturbed by a malicious presence. Sheila described a nasty male spirit. She described this man as weak in the legs and that he suffered from heart palpitations. She said he was "not all there". He was disturbed, "weird" and exuded a strong negative presence. She said he did odd things to animals and was into taxidermy. He liked to pull things apart with his hands and he liked to intimidate people. He spent a lot of his time in a creepy basement with dirt floors like something from the movie "Silence of the Lambs". Sheila put up a psychic barrier around the garage to keep the dark spirit away from the owner's property. She did confirm this spirit was attached to the land around the house but it was not attached to the garage or the owner's home.

Hopefully, the occupants of this home can sleep at night knowing that they are protected by a friendly guard dog in the house and the dark spirit can no longer trespass on their land.

2 King St. N
Ultimate Healing Concepts

In 1949 a talented carpenter, Henry Reed, built a white stucco house on this land that also encompassed the wood building behind it. Before the house was built it was the site of the town's skating rink and a dog pound. After the house was built Henry himself lived in it. He sold it in 1970. It became a real estate office for a short time and then it was sold again to another couple. Currently, Sheila Trecartin and her business Ultimate Healing Concepts occupy the building.

When Sheila moved in, she discovered the building came with one male spirit who was attached to the farm land years before Henry Reed bought the property and built his house in 1949. This spirit from the mid 1800's was much more active before Sheila moved into the space. He is pretty quiet with her and keeps to himself but she is able to communicate with him and has asked him to please keep it down when she has clients. She keeps the energy at a certain level and she says he is respectful and does not usually intrude but sometimes when she is working with people doing a healing with the CD player, the sound will go up and up and the lights will flicker. That is him, she said.

Cate had to book an appointment to see Sheila in order to interview her about the ghost in her store, her business and her life as a medium. Sheila has such a great reputation and is so popular as a medium, healer and animal communicator that people usually have to wait at least 2 months before they can see her after they call for an appointment.

Sheila said she was a child when she first began to feel spirit around her but she was so terrified she would push them away and say, "NO!" when they came to her. She learned to block them out. She would often sleep on the bed with a circle of stuffed animals around her for protection. Sheila lived in a haunted house in Northern Ontario where spirits came to her, closet doors and the attic door would close and open on their own, lights and the radio would turn on and off on their own. She remembers one time when her father was at the dinner table and was making fun of a picture of his father-in-law, she saw a fork literally fly off the table and fall on his foot. Her father stopped laughing after that.

At 12, Sheila began to see auras around people. She also

started getting visions. She had a very clear vision of her cousin being murdered. She saw everything that happened to her. Tragically, her cousin was raped and stabbed to death by her stepfather. The girl was only 12 years old. Sheila also had a vision of where they would find her body.

Sheila was engaged early to her high school sweetheart. At 16 she had a vision that he was going to die soon. He died in September of that year. One time she saw his spirit walk towards her when she was in the house. He disappeared when she started to cry. It was too upsetting for her to see him. She said to this day he sends her images of doves to let her know he is around her.

At 18, Sheila knew she was empathic. She sensed or felt a spirit first and then came levels of seeing and hearing them. At that point she decided that something positive had to come from her ability and she wanted to help people who had lost loved ones. She began studying the holistic field. Her psychic abilities grew stronger during this period. By the time she opened a New Age store at the age of 27, she was clearly seeing and hearing those in the spirit world.

Sheila remembered being in a book club a year prior to opening her store. They were reading The Celestine Prophecy. She looked up and saw a male spirit standing behind a woman in the book club. The man identified himself to Sheila as the woman's husband and he wanted Sheila to tell his wife that he didn't like the picture she hung up in the house of him. She put up a formal, posed picture of him and he wanted the picture where he was carefree and walking on a path in Europe. His wife knew exactly what Sheila was talking about. She was never sure about the picture she did put up and was going home to change it to the picture taken in Europe. Sheila said that was the first time she had ever acknowledged a spirit in that way and passed on a message to a loved one. Today, she is an old pro at this.

At that point, Cate wanted to know if she could talk to the spirit who was in Sheila's store. Sheila told Cate he stayed in the basement but she called him upstairs so he could answer questions. Sheila said he was attached to the property and wore a farmer's hat and clothing and suspenders. She picked up that he was on the land in the 1850's to early 1860's. Sheila said he respected her needs and protected her place. He was guarding her property. He believes he is the caretaker of the land that he once farmed. Sheila stated he was reserved and didn't like to give out a lot of private information.

With that in mind, Cate asked the spirit about his family. Sheila communicated the question to the spirit telepathically. She said he had a daughter that was very important to him. She medically assisted with the delivery of babies. She was a midwife and did a lot of work with healing herbs. He said his daughter's name was Jennifer or Jenna. He said his wife named Emily died before him in 1857 and that he passed from the chest and throat in the 1870's. He said his name was Fred and he talked about his connection to the Williams family. He told us he had a brother named

Bill and he was not stuck but chose to be here and he could leave when he wanted too.

Fred said he didn't like all the people coming and going from Sheila's store but he was respectful of Sheila and he could relate to her. He said she was like his daughter in that they were both healers and did a lot of good for others. After that, Fred left the upstairs sitting room and went back downstairs to the basement. The interview was over before it barely began! Sheila was correct. Fred did not like to give out a lot of private information!

To check out the full range of holistic services that Sheila offers to people and pets, look up her website at www.sheilatrecartin.com

Image courtesy of the Cookstown Women's Institute, Tweedsmuir History

16B Wellington St.
The Old Train Station

The train station was built in Cookstown in 1879. A railroad line running through the west side of town allowed the village to flourish until the 1960's. The railroad transported passengers, wheat, cotton, flour and other goods and staples. Cookstown was a major supplier of cotton for the soldiers fighting overseas during WW2.

The land itself also had a house on it. In 1897 that house was moved to the opposite side of the street. Built in its place was a large evaporator factory. This factory dried apples. Local farmers would take their apples to the factory and they would be dried on strings. The apples could be purchased by the string or in a barrel.

The back of the house still has the platform.

The train station itself closed in 1967. The station was then renovated and made into a semi-detached house. The actual railroad line was later converted into a section of the Trans-Canada Trail.

In 2010, Kim Turtscher and her family moved into 16B Wellington Street. Kim, affectionately known as Miss Kim around town, moved into the home because she loved the fact that it was once the old train station. She also loved the energy of the home. She showed us part of the original platform with heavy wooden beams and the original dark, thick and wide wood plank flooring.

Kim stated when her daughter was fairly young, she spent one night in the basement bedroom and complained that she could not sleep in there because she heard too many ghostly voices in the night.

When we entered the house, we were both overcome with

a rush of residual energy from all the busy traffic that was once part of the station. As we entered the basement bedroom, we sensed a strong male presence, possibly a caretaker of the station at one time.

Image courtesy of the Cookstown Women's Institute, Tweedsmuir History

Later, we brought medium Sheila Trecartin with us to investigate the old train station.

As we parked the car by the old rail line which is now part of the Trans-Canada Trail, Sheila picked up on the spirits of two young railroad workers about the age of 19 or 20 years old. One of these rail workers died of heat stroke/ exhaustion but they keep each other company as they linger outside the property and walk along the trail together.

Inside the old building, Sheila picked up a male spirit who was very stern and controlling. He was concerned about time and the whole station. He was a former time keeper for the trains. He lived close by and would walk to work. This was the spirit we picked up on in the basement earlier.

Sheila also picked up another male spirit from the 1970's. She said he was an older gentleman who wore high knee socks. He was ill with diabetes. He was one of the original owners when the train station was converted into homes. When Sheila asked what he did, he replied, "not much" and then he said the care of the property was very important to him and he would frequently cut the grass.

Kim certainly has nothing to worry about from these four male spirits who continue to watch over and take care of the old train station and the property.

As we were parked on the road beside the old station, the spirit of a little 5 year old boy approached the car. He told Sheila that he had drowned and he talked of a well. He said he had an older sister who was 7 or 8 years old and he was looking for his sister and was waiting for her. This boy was cute but mischievous and told Sheila he liked to play games on people. He talked about the school he attended with his sister. The old school was built in 1888 and was located right beside the busy train station. In 1961, the school was sold to Triboro Quilt Co. Ltd. who manufactured baby clothes. The factory closed in 1967, the same year the train station closed.

Sheila tried to talk to the little boy and get him to move on to the light but he laughed and thought it was a trick. Sheila said he was not ready to leave yet.

At that point, a female spirit appeared. She identified her-self to Sheila as the custodian or caretaker of the old school and said that she had been a teacher at the school since it opened. Sheila described her. She wore a bun, had buck teeth and was a spinster. In her hand was a school bell she would ring. The teacher pointed out the well the 5 year old boy was talking about. It was once behind the old train station and close to the old school. Sheila said this spirit was sad and longed for her old life as a teacher. Her whole life revolved around the school and the children and she missed those days.

After the conversation ended, the teacher disappeared and the little boy waved good-bye as we drove away.

Image courtesy of the Bradford West Gwillimbury Pubic Library

The old school

Just outside Cookstown

Queens Hotel
Thornton

Thornton lies just to the north of Cookstown on Highway 27. Around 1850, Thornton was just a small village. The Queen's Hotel was owned by Irish settler, John Stewart at that time and acted as a rest stop for weary travellers headed north. Over the years, it also served as a group home as well as a restaurant.

The old 19th century inn has long had a reputation of being

haunted by locals. The ghost story dates back to the 1890's when the Queen's Hotel was at its height as a roadside inn. The following account of the haunting was written in the Barrie Advance in October 2009:

"In the village of Thornton, a former hotel serves up fine fare under the watchful gaze of a tragic female spectre. The Thornton Village Inn is a beautifully nostalgic Victorian building and a fine dining establishment, its pleasing appearance and excellent food masking the dark stains of a terrible crime.

During the 19th century, the building was host to many travelers, but among the masses one pair, a young couple, stood out. She was beautiful and gentle, he abusive and unfeeling. One night, the woman and her cruel husband began to quarrel, and as it often did, the fight soon turned violent. The woman fell under a rain of insults and punches that left her body and spirit bruised. She was either thrown down the stairs from the second floor or fell as she ran from the assault. In either case, by the time her body had come to rest at the bottom, it was broken and lifeless.

Since then, "The Lady of the Stairs" is said to haunt the second floor of the restaurant. She can be seen standing atop the staircase, walking along the second-floor mezzanine, and looking mournfully down upon the village below from the second-floor balcony. Tradition states she appears most often on the anniversary of her death."

One afternoon as the former manager of the hotel sat with his cook before opening, the two heard footsteps above them on the second floor. Being the only two in the restaurant, they immediately took to the staircase. No intruder was found. Upon further investigation, it was discovered that the footsteps were heard in the room directly beside the stairs where it was said the couple fought.

The haunted mezzanine

A waitress who currently works at the LOL café in Cookstown, once worked at the old Inn in Thornton when it was a restaurant. She had many stories to tell about this ghost lady. The waitress said this ghost would move objects in the kitchen and she could often hear her walking upstairs when no one else was in the building. Customers would often make reports of a shadow figure on the stairs.

In the book, "More Ontario Ghost Stories", Maria Da Silva and Andrew Hind have reported the following two accounts of the ghost of the old Queen's Hotel:

The first incident occurred years ago. A couple dining for the evening found the service, the ambience and the food absolutely delightful. It was, in all respects, a perfect evening, except for the strange lady who kept peering at them through the glass doors on the second floor. "The woman was distinct and appeared tangible and very real. When we first saw her looking at us through the door, we didn't think too much of it. It's only when it persisted that we started to think it rude and a little creepy. Finally, I thought enough was enough, and I made a complaint about the leering woman. The colour literally drained from the waitress' face. There was no other women staff members on duty that night and there should have been no one on the second floor. Those doors were locked and inaccessible, so no one could possibly be in there. The woman staring out from behind the door all night, therefore, could only have been a ghost."

The second incident occurred in October 2005. A couple parked their car in the pouring rain and made a mad dash for the front door. They looked up at the balcony above the doorway and saw standing there a forlorn woman looking out upon the village. She wore only a thin dress but seemed unmoved by the foul weather. The woman looked so sad and tragic. For a brief moment their eyes met and an oppressive chill ran through them. The vision of the woman haunted them throughout the meal. When the woman in the party excused herself and headed to the bathroom, she heard footsteps and felt someone follow her. The woman was at the bathroom sink when she again heard heeled footsteps approaching from behind. It sounded like another woman was in the bathroom with her but when she looked around she discovered she was very much alone. Still, the footsteps continued to approach, slowly and purposefully. The closer the footsteps came, the stronger the ghost's presence could be felt. The footsteps stopped directly behind her. After that, the woman ran out the door in terror. The romantic dinner came to an abrupt end.

Medium Sheila Trecartin confirmed that this spirit does exist. She has seen her or felt her on a number of occasions when she has dined in the restaurant in the past. Sheila states there are other spirits in the building as well especially on the third floor and around the fire escape. However, the lady on the stairs continues to be the star attraction at this haunted location.

Front Stairs

In April 2014, the old Queen's Hotel changed ownership. Kim Vidya, a yoga teacher, holistic nutritionist and natural health practitioner opened a vegetarian restaurant as well as a yoga and wellness center at this location. The Veggie Gourmet is the only organic and gluten free vegetarian restaurant in this area and the great food is out of this world, just like the spirits in the building!

Kim said the old hotel completely drew her in when she first saw it. She explained she wanted to create a healthy alternative in the area. She wanted a community social gathering place where kindred spirits felt pampered and supported. She was very aware that there were spirits in the building. She had encounters with the "lady on the stairs" and found the energies in the building to be heavy and stagnant when she first arrived. Kim had another medium come to the old hotel and she said there was a portal where spirits would come and go. This medium said there were two male spirits on the third floor. They told the medium they would leave shortly. At one point, an 80 year old woman came to the restaurant. She told Kim that her father and her uncle once owned this building and they both died in it. When Kim described the two male spirits to this woman, she was convinced it was her father and her uncle.

Kim has been working on clearing the heavy and stagnant energies in the building and has found the atmosphere becoming clearer and less congested. There is a lighter feeling when you walk into the building now. Even the spirits seem happier in this new healthy environment with good food and healing practices.

When Cate took a tour of the building, she could feel the presence of the woman walking behind her while she was upstairs on the mezzanine. Her energy was very strong. Cate stood on the same spot on the balcony where the woman has been spotted in the past. A pressure feeling surrounded her and overwhelmed Cate and she had to stand back because the sensation was too intense to stay there for long. She also had a brief vision of the woman.

While having lunch downstairs, Cate glanced over to the portrait of a woman above the fireplace. "It's her!" she exclaimed. It was the image of the woman that came to her mind when she was on the balcony. This spirit had long brown hair, was pale and thin and wore a long dark dress. Although the painting was modern, it captured the essence of the 19th century woman. Subconsciously, someone had picked out a painting of "the lady on the stairs" without even realizing it and hung it over the fireplace. Cate gets shivers every time she sees it.

Cherry Valley Farm
Thornton

Just down the road from The Veggie Gourmet in Thornton is a little known hot spot of spirit activity. The following article about Cherry Valley Farm was written by Cate Crow and appeared in The Innisfil Scope on June 5, 2013:

Angels, Native Spirit Guides, Ghosts and the Largest Portal in Canada

Just north of Cookstown on the outskirts of the village of Thornton lies a spiritual healing oasis, a hidden gem in the countryside of Simcoe County. Cherry Valley Farm on the 10th Line was opened to the public by the owner, Nancy Fletcher Huber, in the summer of 2007. This modest white farmhouse and the 100 acres of farmland which surround it have been labelled sacred by a number of medicine men and women, mediums and spiritual healers over the years.

Once land that was settled on by the Ojibwa natives, it was purchased by the Fletcher family who emigrated from Cherry Valley, Ireland in 1844. The original log cabin which was built on the property by John Thompson Fletcher, the first treasurer of Simcoe County, has since been replaced by the white farmhouse which was built in 1900 by Maitland Fletcher for his bride Leila. Maitland and Leila were Nancy's grandparents. At the same time he built the house, Maitland planted the beautiful large Carolina Poplars that can be seen towering over the farmhouse today.

Nancy inherited the farm in 2000 and for three years planted organic garlic on the land. A gifted medium who works with Archangel Raphael, Nancy realized the incredible energy that was coming from the land itself. For years, Nancy had done remote viewing absent healing, otherwise known as distant healing, with a group of friends at the farm. She was in the field when she realized that the energy coming from the house and land itself would make a perfect place to gather healers and light workers to do spiritual healing energy work.

After restoring the farm to its former glory after years of neglect, Nancy with the help of Sheila Trecartin of Ultimate Healing Concepts in Cookstown and her daughter-in-law Yvette Huber, a gifted Reiki Master, opened the doors for business. Over 14 energy vortexes/portals have been discovered on the immediate property surrounding the house with many more discovered in the outlying fields. According to NoraWalksinSpirit and Algonquin Shaman Peter Bernard, along with mediums Karen Egoff and Sheila Trecartin and remote viewer Richard Bryant, these vortexes and portals are connected to and contain the same spiritual energy found at sacred sites across the planet including Machu Picchu, Ancient Egypt, The crystal peaks of the Himalayas, Stonehenge, Glastonbury, Sedona etc. When Nancy asked Pete Bernard why there were so many spirits on the land, he said, "What do you expect? With these vortexes, it's like an airport here." Nancy has been told that her property is protected by 40 angels and native spirit guides. Even her ancestors haunt the farm.

The largest portal in Canada is located behind the barn at Cherry Valley. In the front of the barn lies a crystal medicine wheel several feet below the ground. The energy here is truly intense. As Nora WalksinSpirit stated, "We have no understanding of why this farm in Canada but there is a crystal medicine wheel in the ground and it is massive. There are certain pivotal portals on the planet that are coming together and this portal on this farm is really significant!"

A spiritual labyrinth can be walked at the farm. It was built in yet another healing portal on the land. The seven circuit design corresponds to the seven sacred chakra centers of the body.
Walking this land is truly an incredible experience with

the kind of sacred energy that it exudes. Nancy's ancestors have made appearances in both the field and the house, along with the spirit native warriors who guard the property. Some have even had visions of Jesus and Mary by the barn. Karen Egoff who works with the angelic realm said, "You don't have to go to Sedona or travel anywhere else to experience portals. They are right here!" She also said, "Miracles will happen on this land" and indeed many have as Nancy will tell you. Nancy is currently writing a second book on the miracles that have happened and continue to happen at Cherry Valley. She recently published her first book, "Synchronicities" about the healing retreat and it is now available at the farm, The Bell, Book and Candle in Barrie and Windspirit in Orillia.

Today, Cherry Valley is a private residence that offers weekend tours of the labyrinth and portals on certain dates. The farm also offers a number of weekend workshops including divine Reiki energy levels 1, 2 and Master Reiki; Connecting with your Angels and Spirit Guides; Gifting of the Munay Ki Rites, Animal Communications and Animal Totem Workshops, Past Life Regression among many other healing modalities designed to help you find the spiritual path you came here to walk.

To learn more about Cherry Valley Retreat, check out the following website www.cherryvalleyretreat.com

Nancy Fletcher Huber will tell you all about the spirits on her property. Her grandfather Maitland and great, great grandfather John Thompson have made appearances to several people on the land. Her grandmother Leila, her great grandmother Orpha and Orpha's husband Frank have made appearances to people in the farmhouse along with her own father, Arthur Fletcher. Native spirits have also been seen on the property.

Cate experienced her relatives after she stayed overnight at the farmhouse. This account comes from Nancy's book, Synchronicities, "After I hooked up with Cate Crow, who volunteered to edit my book, we had a meeting and dinner at the farm. Cate stayed over in the guest bedroom which is closest to the landing. While trying to sleep, she heard many voices and had to put her finger in her ear to shut out the noise. She was woken at 5:55 am by someone pacing and making noise outside the door of her room. She thought it must have been me and opened the door. There was no one there and the pacing stopped. The pacing started again after she went back to bed. She said the noises didn't stop until she heard me get up. I never feel anything but safe and protected at the farm but that makes sense because it is my relatives who guard the place."

Cate wrote the following account of another experience in the house, "I left the living room and went to use the washroom upstairs. When I went to leave the bathroom, someone tried to push open the door. I pushed back. I thought I must have startled the poor person who was obviously desperate to use the washroom and didn't know I was in there. I opened the door to apologize and found no one was there. Everyone was still downstairs. Nancy had told me there were spirits of her ancestors in her home, especially on the second floor, and I realized I had just encountered one of them!" When Cate told this story to Nancy, she said others have had the exact same experience in the washroom. She also said some clients have been afraid of going up the stairs. They feel a presence guarding the landing who doesn't want them on the second floor.

The first time Amy Woodcock came to the farm, she knew nothing about spirits in the house or on the land. She came to take a tour of the land. She writes, "At the house I felt energy as soon as I entered the back porch. The most energy was on the landing of the stairs, like someone was there. Before we started the tour, while standing in our circle, I felt many, many, many spirits around us." She went upstairs to use the washroom and came down and asked Nancy if she was aware that there were ghosts on the second floor. She said she had a never ending head rush until she came down the stairs.

Yvette Huber, Nancy's daughter-in-law had another visitation in the night and asked Nancy, "Did you have a pair of ancestors, one who was a very tall large man and another who was a small woman?" Nancy confirmed that she did. It was her great grandmother Orpha and her husband Frank. Yvette said she had woken during the night and saw them standing over the bed just watching over her and her husband Ken (Nancy's son). Yvette said she felt no fear, only a feeling of protection. She closed and opened her eyes again a few times and they were still there.

Nancy told us that at one time there was a young man staying at the house who kicked in one of the panels of a downstairs door in a fit of temper. She said he was a big man standing at just over 6'5" and was very heavy. During his sleep at Cherry Valley, he was literally booted out of bed onto the floor by an unseen presence. He now says, "That farm is haunted" and refuses to come back. Nancy feels it was the spirit of her father Arthur, who was angry at the man for destroying the door of his former home.

Sheila Trecartin has had several encounters with the spirits at Cherry Valley. She sees many native male warrior spirits guarding the land. Sheila teaches courses at the farm and the first time she was in the house without Nancy, she said the spirits really challenged her presence and wanted her to leave. She said they gradually came to accept her and no longer bother her when she comes to teach. Nancy and others often hear these spirits coming up the stairs to the back porch and back door but when they look outside, no one is there.

At one of Sheila's Animal Totems classes, a lady sitting near the doorway to the downstairs hall said, "There is someone standing here just outside the doorway". There was no one there but Sheila said, "I know and I've asked her to wait out there until the workshop is done so that we are not disturbed". It turned out to be the spirit of Nancy's grandmother Leila who wanted the group to keep the noise down, especially the animal spirits Sheila had called in. In other classes, clients have reported seeing Nancy's grandmother sitting in a rocking chair in the living room. Another client saw Nancy's great grandmother Orpha walk through her own portrait in the same room.

Nancy said when another medium was teaching at the farm, she channelled a man coming up from the barn who was saying, "Fix the barn foundations". From her description, she knew it was her grandfather Maitland. Many people have seen Maitland's spirit walking in the fields on the farm. Recently, a group of women who attended an Angel workshop went for a walk on the property after the course was over. They split into two groups. One woman in each group saw an old man in the field and wondered who he was. They were completely shocked and surprised when the other women in their group said they couldn't see an old man and said there was no one in the field. He was clear as a bell to the two women who obviously had psychic gifts. An Ojibwa native named James told Nancy he saw an old man on the porch with Nancy one afternoon and confirmed for her that it was her grandfather's spirit.

During an open house at the farm in June 2013, Nora Walkinspirit did medicine wheel teachings around the medicine wheel in the field. There were over 100 people in the circle during the teachings. When the teaching was over and everyone left the circle, a 15 year old psychic girl said she saw 5 spirits remain around the circle. She described two native male warriors, two Indian children and an old man. From the description she gave of the old man, Nancy knew it was her grandfather Maitland.

In the woods to the north of the farm is a depression where the original log cabin was built in the mid 1800's by John Thompson Fletcher, Nancy's great, great grandfather. A gentleman was on a tour of the portals and labyrinth of the property when he went into the woods. He was sitting in the Gaia chalice portal meditating when he looked up and saw a ghostly male spirit in 19th century clothing coming from the direction of the old log cabin. He could see his clothing with suspenders but he could not see a face on the man. He thought he was hallucinating and went to shake his head. When he looked up again, this ghostly figure was standing in front of him and said quite clearly, "What are you doing on my land?" After that, the spirit completely disappeared.

If you plan to visit the farm, check with the website first to find out when workshops or tours of the property are being offered. The website also provides directions to the retreat.

Museum on the Boyne
Alliston

Just to the west of Cookstown is the town of Alliston. Alliston is best known as the home of Dr. Frederick Banting, the man who discovered insulin in the 1920's. However, among ghost hunters, Alliston is better known as the home of the haunted Museum on the Boyne. The Museum has been investigated by a number of mediums and paranormal groups over the years. The following newspaper reports have been published about this location:

From the Shelburne Free Press:

Paranormal activity at the Museum on the Boyne
The paranormal world is widely disputed. There are some who strongly believe in the presence of unseen spirits

around us every day, some who adamantly disbelieve, and then some who are on the fence.

The popularity of the subject, however, cannot be disputed. Countless movies including the Paranormal Activity series and Insidious continue to entertain thrill seeking movie-goers, terrified of the unknown. A tidal wave of reality television shows about ghost hunting has also flooded cable channels.

Clearly curiosity exists.

For Shelburne woman Tara MacDougall, getting people to give in to their curiosity is one of the biggest parts of her job. MacDougall is the owner and operator of the South Western Ontario Paranormal Society, created in 2010. She partnered with other investigators to conduct an in-vestigation at the local Museum on the Boyne in Alliston. MacDougall was joined by her sister Krista Johnston, Mark and Trevor Bishop-Larocque of the Ontario Gay Paranor-mal Society and Wanda Hewer, an independent certified paranormal investigator, Psychic-Medium, Paranormal Consultant and founder of Ghost Hunters of Guelph. My editor Wendy Gabrek and I were able to go along for the experience.

The museum was built in 1914, and originally used as an Agricultural Fair building. The barn on the property was built in 1858, and the log cabin built in 1851. The cabin was one of the first artifact donations to the museum, a building that was moved there from Essa as an attraction. The museum features a permanent collection of approximately 5000 items, plus additional items from travelling collections that are featured twice a year.

The museum has been the subject of a number of investigations over the years for paranormal activity because of several sightings claimed by different people. Based on its high level of paranormal activity, the Museum on the Boyne is rated 8.5 out of 10.

Museum curator Katie Huddleston confirms that strange happenings do occur, having experienced some herself. A Medium investigating the museum at one time told her that spirits are typically very respectful, and you can ask them not to show themselves if you are afraid of them. Huddleston says she has had seen shadows move on the upper level balcony inside.

Other strange things have been known to happen as well, like old clocks chiming suddenly, even though they haven't been working for years and the old piano making noise as if someone played a key. Sounds of a baby crying have also been reported coming from the old cabin.

"Everyone likes to investigate at nighttime because it's quieter on the street and everything, but we have activity at all hours of the day," says Huddleston.

She considers herself to have a respectful coexistence with

the spirits in the museum, but says she hears a lot especially when she is there alone after hours.

"I still hate going to the cabin by myself," Huddleston admits.

The investigation with South Western Ontario Paranormal Society revealed the spirit of an angry man and child in the cabin, and the investigators were able to communicate with at least one child inside the museum. It wasn't determined if it was the same child in both places.

Activity was detected by video cameras that were monitored by one of the investigators, as well as different instruments that use light as indicators. The colour of lights on those tools changed depending on temperature, so outside on that frigid winter night the light would turn blue, normal temperature showed green lights and higher than normal showed red lights.

Some of the investigators were able to communicate with the child spirit by asking "yes" or "no" questions. For example, they asked the spirit if it was a boy and the light changed from green to red, indicating a yes. No change in the lights meant that the answer was no, or that the spirit was no longer communicating.

There was no activity detected in the barn, but when we explored the cabin the investigators described a hostile male spirit, a drunk, to be occupying the space.

Certain images believed to contain spirits were taken from different digital cameras at the time.

While conducting an EVP session (Electronic Voice Phenomenon) in the cabin, MacDougall asked several questions to the child spirit as well as the older male. Investigators say the digital voice recorders sometimes pick up additional voices than the living people in the room, voices that make sounds and respond to their questions in single words or sometimes a full sentence.

Huddleston says many EVP sessions have been conducted in the museum before, and in one a strange, unidentified sound similar to a neighing horse could be heard. At one time there was a horse racing track next to the museum, when it was still used as an Agricultural Farm building. Before the EVP session, Wendy Gabrek, Editor of the Shelburne Free Press, The Innisfil Scope and the Times of New Tecumseth, connected with a spirit in the cabin. She described what was happening at the time as she had the distinct feeling that a child was clinging to her leg on the upper level of the building, while at the same time her brand new flashlight faded off and on repeatedly.

I was in the room with her at the time, as well as investigator Mark Bishop-Larocque. He asked me if I could feel anything, but I was unaware of any presence apart from the people I could see. What I felt was a strong sense of calm. Later, however, when we conducted the EVP session, I sometimes had the distinct feeling that something was looming directly behind me, the feeling you get when a tall man stands behind you.

Before the investigation began, Wanda Hewer of Ghost Hunters of Guelph led us in an exercise of meditation, meant to open our minds to the experience. My mind was open, and I am a believer, but unfortunately I don't think I experienced the presence of spirits in the same way as the others, as much as I wanted to.

But there were still a few things that happened that made me believe I had witnessed paranormal activity that night. First, at the beginning of the evening I was seated next to Wendy when the DSLR camera in her lap snapped a picture on its own. It happened while someone was asking a child spirit questions, and the lighted instruments on the floor with us were responding rapidly. There were other strange things happening to the technology, something Huddleston says is not uncommon in that building for investigators. The video feeds in the back room of the museum showed different areas of the museum, where the cameras picked up the sight of dust orbs in the unlit rooms. But those dust orbs are said to be different from spirit orbs, which are perfect circles and move differently. Watching those screens, I could see when a spirit orb moved through the room. Mark and Trevor Bishop-Larocque streamed the entire investigation live on their website, with a chat room for people to ask questions to either the investigators or the spirits.

MacDougall's sister Krista Johnston said she had a vision of a young boy with dark hair and wearing a hat, a description that curator Huddleston said employees at the museum had heard on more than one occasion. She gave two examples of children participating in museum activities who asked about a boy who wasn't joining in. The boy met the description Johnston gave, and could only be seen by those children.

"If you go into an investigation with a loving attitude then you're going to get the kids and the loving spirits," says MacDougall. "It's all about the trust between the living and the dead."

It wasn't the first time the Museum on the Boyne has been investigated, and it won't be the last. As for the South Western Ontario Paranormal Society and her partners, they have plenty of investigations ahead of them.

By Emily Wood

From The New Tecumseth Times:
The ghosts of Simcoe County
August 21, 2013

I discovered the Haunted Barrie Meetup Group and joined them after I moved to Barrie from Toronto. They are the "Ghost Hunters" of this area with an impressive collection of professional ghost tracking equipment to aid in their investigations. The group was formed by Jeff Ostrander in

2007. Jeff is no stranger to investigating and documenting reported haunted locations throughout Canada and the United States. Tara VanderMeulen has been with the group from the beginning and is now the public relations manager and assistant organizer for events. There are currently over 600 ghost enthusiasts who are members of this "spirited" organization.

I recently sat down with Tara to discuss Simcoe County's ghostly hot spots:

The Museum on the Boyne
The Museum on the Boyne (or the "BOO"yne) in Alliston features a collection of haunted buildings. There is the MacDonald Log Cabin dated 1851, the 1858 English Barn as well as the 1914 Agricultural Fair Building. According to Tara, there have been many strange occurrences that have happened in these buildings over the years. Activity in the museum ranges from loud stomps across the floors, a blue haze traveling across the back room, an unexplained cold presence, display cases flung open and artifacts removed, display cases rearranged and unknown lights and orbs spotted in the attic of the main museum, the barn and the first floor of the cabin.

Katie, the Curator, is very familiar with the spirit of "Andrew", an older gentleman who once worked in the building but who now frequents the attic and balcony. There are the "Lovely Ladies" who appear every June in high heels for a dance or social occasion of some kind and then disappear shortly after. There is also a ghost cat that has been seen wandering around the first floor of the main building. In the cabin are the sinister MacDonald boys. Psychics have described "Angus" as an angry sort who does not like women with long dark hair. In the past, women who fit this description have described an uneasy feeling, have felt a pressure on their back and have even been pushed. An apparition of a hand was witnessed in the log cabin followed by a loud bang on the first floor table. In one EVP (electronic voice phenomenon) session in the cabin, a male voice was heard saying, "Get Out" to a group of women investigators followed by the "B" word. Another EVP captured the sound of a baby crying. There are cold chill spots throughout the cabin and compasses have been known to go haywire in there. During a strictly controlled audio recording session in the cabin, unknown male voices were heard talking over top of Jeff, while a loud bang sound from the loom was captured on camera.

By Cate Crow

Cate was involved in an investigation of the Museum on the Boyne with the Haunted Barrie Meetup Group in March 2013. She recalls the EMF jumping from a scale of O to 5 when she pointed the device at the back wall of the Agricultural building. The group captured strange orbs and lights in the attic where Andrew is said to reside. The cabin felt very creepy. A woman with long hair sitting opposite Cate at the table felt her hair constantly being touched. Her friend Mary reported hearing "Get Out" followed by the

"B" word on the EVP that night after Cate left to go home for the evening.

Cate Crow (second from left) getting ready for a night investigating the haunted Museum on the Boyne with the Haunted Barrie Meetup Group

Mary keeps a close eye on the monitors for any sign of activity

Another article from the Barrie Examiner:
Alliston museum a beacon for spirits and those who believe

Barrie Examiner
October 30, 2013

Dead fall leaves crunch under-foot as you make your way to the centuries-old wooden door of the cabin at the Museum on the Boyne in Alliston.

Opening the heavy door, the smell of old, dry wood greets the visitor as their eyes adjust from the bright sunlight to the natural light inside the cabin. Set back from the museum's main building, the small Scottish home circa 1800s was roughly hewn from timber felled by hand long ago. At any other time of year, the old loom, furniture and quilting would be appreciated for their quality craftsmanship. But in late October, we're here to listen for ghosts. Tara VanderMeulen, 39, a paranormal investigator with the Haunted Barrie Meetup Group, has brought a digital recorder and headphones with her as she has done before.

The sensible woman with red curly hair under the large headphones records everything going on in the room, and will listen to what the recorder picks up when she gets home. That's how she heard the baby crying. The meet-up group had set up cameras in the cabins with live screens watched in the main building.

A half-dozen people sat around the sturdy harvest table in the cabin and asked a question, waited 20 seconds or so and then asked another. Later, when VanderMeulen was reviewing the tape, she could very faintly hear a newborn baby crying in the silence on the recorder.

"The psychic woman we had with us said she could sense a woman was busy cooking in the cabin and there were children around," VanderMeulen said. "We heard the baby crying at about 12:30 a.m. It was October and cold and late. We didn't hear it while we were there, only after when I listened to the recording.

"She hasn't seen ghosts or spirits in the main building at the museum, but has felt a cat brush up against her leg and heard footsteps as if people are walking around on the wooden floors. One of the best paranormal moments happened in 2010 when they were looking at an old Victorian-styled wicker coffin display.
"A (group) member said, 'Ew, you'd be able to see the body in there through the holes' and this really crazy weird sound, almost like a horse whinny or a death rattle in someone's chest was heard," VanderMeulen said.

"I've never heard anything like that before or since." Psychic Lynn Jankowski, 48, has visited the cabin behind the museum a number of times. She said she's seen dead people since she was a child, but only recently began admitting to people she was in touch with spirits.

She remembers as a young child waking up before 5 a.m. one morning and seeing her grandfather standing at the bottom of her bed. The family received a call later that day that he had died the night before.

Jankowski said she stood on the museum's cabin's second-floor bedroom area and sensed a young girl around the age of 10.

"I was standing up there and I heard a soft groan and the ground sort of shifted beneath my feet," she said, motioning as if jumping to maintain her balance.

The museum doesn't seem to mind the haunted sightings heard over the years. In fact, staff have experienced enough haunting moments to believe in the paranormal phenomena themselves.

The museum's heritage co-ordinator, Katie Huddleston, had her first brush with spirits when she took the position six years ago.

"I came in and made some changes to one of the displays. I was new and a little gung-ho to make my mark, I guess. So I changed some things around and when I came in the next morning, everything I'd moved was sitting on the floor. It had all been taken off the shelves and it's as if I was being told, 'this is not how we do things here'," she said with a laugh.

"There's lots of see out-of-the-corner-of-your-eye stuff and you think, 'Was that something?', or you'll hear one single note played quietly on the piano and then it's gone. There are no apparitions to scare you just lots of things that make you go, hmmm."

By Cheryl Browne

Times Newspaper
Beeton

Recently, Wendy Gabrek, the editor of the Innisfil Scope, the New Tecumseth Times and the Shelburne Free Press wrote to Cate and Amy asking if they would like to join her in an investigation of the Times newspaper building on the main street of Beeton. Beeton lies just to the south of Cookstown. This building was erected in 1894 and has been used for many purposes over the years. It was an opera, town hall, farmers' market, hardware store and is currently used as a news room.

The investigation took place on the evening of Friday August 15, 2014 and included Cate, Amy, medium Sheila Trecartin, medium Trish Hubel, Wendy Gabrek, and her co-workers John Speziali and Lisa Clendening . Lisa brought her daughter Sarah Hyde.

As we all gathered in the front of the Times, the sun began to set. Wendy informed us we would be investigating the third floor which has been closed to the public for years and the first floor of the newsroom. The second floor contained an apartment and was off limits.

The following are the notes Cate took that evening:

When medium Sheila Trecartin walked into the building she focused on Sarah Hyde, daughter of Lisa, a graphic artist at The Times. Sheila said she had music all around her. Sarah confirmed she was a classical musician and played piano, guitar, the ukulele and sang. Music was her life and her passion. There was nothing Sarah was wearing or anything she had on her that would indicate she was a musician.

Medium Sheila Trecartin communicating with the spirits

Upstairs on the third floor, Sheila picked up the spirit of a Victorian woman who claimed ownership of the building and land. This spirit was very stern, hard, structured and unsettled. She was wearing a hat with a feather. Her hair was done up and pinned. She was well dressed, immaculate in appearance. She said this land belonged to her family. Sheila picked up that her father was either the first or second owner. When her father died suddenly, she felt injustice at how hard she had to fight to show/maintain ownership of the property but men took over and it was sold. She picked up the name Beth or Bethany.

Amy Woodcox is surrounded by spirit orbs while taking pictures

On the third floor she also picked up the spirit of a man who was working on the building on a scaffold, when he fell and died. She also picked up the spirit of a man who died in the 1980's. He was short with dark hair and a pronounced jawline. He was a car salesman in life. He died abruptly and was somehow linked to the building. She picked up the name of Watson and was not sure if it belonged to this spirit or the spirit of the worker who fell and died.

Sheila picked up that there was a huge bat infestation on the third floor at one time. Wendy confirmed that at one time the windows in the building were all broken and there were pigeons and bats and animals up on the third floor.

Sheila picked up that there was a lot of socializing, music and dancing on the third floor. This room was like a ballroom at one time. She also picked up a courtroom downstairs. It was confirmed that people were hung in this building in the past. Wendy was aware of a man who was hung in the building in the late 1800's for stealing cattle.

Sheila felt that there was a strong religious connection/presence on the third floor. She picked up that this room was used as a church at one time after a local church burned down and that there was an old pioneer burial ground at the back of the building dating from the early 1800's. She picked up white tombstones at the back of the building. Currently, there is an addition at the back of this building so any burial ground is under it.

Trish Hubel, another medium, who works as a Remax sales representative compared notes with Sheila from the third floor. She picked up the name Danny, Susanna or "Susie" and Elizabeth (Beth) and said this woman was well dressed and was tough and accepted no bs! This was the same stern, well dressed Victorian woman spirit, "Beth" that Sheila picked up on. Trish felt her family name began with a "B". Trish also picked up "religion" associated with this room and said poor people had their funerals here. Trish also picked up the spirit of Wendy's mother Carol who had passed and just wanted to visit her daughter.

Sarah Hyde was feeling so dizzy by the spiritual energy in the room she had to lean against a wall for support.

On the first floor Cate and Amy both felt a strong presence in the back room on the right side of the building. Sheila picked up a male spirit in a fedora hat. He was a former news reporter connected to the building. He was following Cate around all night, peering over her shoulder to see what she was writing down. Cate felt a strong energy around her left shoulder all night. Cate picked up the name of "John" with this man. Wendy and Lisa laughed and said there were a lot of "John's" associated with this building. Sheila also picked up on a male energy in the back right room. She sensed heartache with this man. This male energy was very sad. She felt his wife had passed and he was very attached to her and was mourning her loss. The female spirit showed Sheila her chest area. Sheila thought she possibly passed from breast cancer. She got an "H" name but was not sure if it was a first, middle or last name and said this man worked here as an employee. She also sensed that there was once a desk at the back of the room and this man once spent a lot of time in the room. Wendy was surprised. Wendy told us that John H. Archibald, the owner of the building, recently lost his wife and this room was once his office and his desk was once located at the back of the room.

Also on the first floor in the front reception room was the spirit of an older lady, rounder in hips, in her 60's who was a secretary and worked in the front room in the late 70's, 80's. Sheila also picked up a nun who took care of sick people and poor people when the building was a town hall or community center of some sort. This building acted as a food bank when there was a famine in the area with not enough to eat.

Lisa explained that one night when she was in the building, she saw a dark shadow figure shuffle across the printing room. Sarah Hyde was spooked by something in the same room that night. Sheila picked up a creepy guy. She described him as a hillbilly type with bad teeth and a slouching posture. He had reddish hair and he liked to hide behind things and tried to scare and intimidate women. He was simple minded and saw woman as play things. Sheila kept picking up the term "rape, pillage and plunder". He was attached to the land. Best to just ignore this guy and he will go away.

Trish picked up an older male spirit in his 60's or 70's named Mike. He was once a caretaker or custodian or groundskeeper of the building and property.

There were other spirits who just came into the building

that evening to see what Sheila and Trish were up too. Sheila explained 2 mediums with an open channel to the other side acted like a beacon and drew spirits to them. A woman spirit from across the road who had cataracts and many cats came into the building and so did a woman who liked to bake fancy cakes. Sadly, a teenage boy who committed suicide came to see Sheila. She described him as a sad, lost soul with long dark hair and a black leather jacket. He was tall and skinny and between 17-20 years old. He died in the 80's and he wanted forgiveness from his parents for what he had done. He said he never meant to hurt them. Sheila reached out and helped this young soul. At one point Sheila said there must have been 300 spirits crowding in The Times building to check out what we were doing that night.

Wendy sent Cate's notes to John Archibald for verification. He wrote, "The only one I can confirm is my name is John H. My wife died of congestive heart failure. The building was built by the municipal government as a town hall and was never privately owned by anyone other than Tom Wood and Bruce Haire and myself".

Sheila said that the Victorian woman was so steadfast that she had to believe that she was connected to this land and felt she owned it.

It is possible that there may have been another building on this property prior to the government building which was constructed in 1894, rather late into the Victorian era when we know Beeton goes back as a settlement to the early 1800's. We found that in Cookstown, older buildings were frequently torn down or destroyed by fire and new ones were built in the same place. Sometimes a spirit was still holding space in the former building. This could have been the case with "Beth" and it is very possible her father owned the land at one time prior to the town hall being built by the municipal government.

Wendy Gabrek's article, "Paranormal investigation reveals more than 300 spirits in Times' building" appeared in The Times newspaper on August 21, 2014.

Spirits & Ghosts
What's the difference?

A visiting spirit is someone who has passed on to the light after they have died but who likes to come back and visit favorite places, family or friends. They are not stuck on the earth plane and can come and go as they please. We ran into many of these souls in Cookstown. There is Chester in Amy's house who loves his old home and likes to hang out there. This is also the case of Mr. Thomas Cooke, the town founder. He loves his old manor home and likes to visit it. This is the case of the woman who loves the theater and loves to sing in the building, the male spirits and female spirit who like to hang out at the Curling Club, Bogdan's aunt and grandfather at the clock shop, Mrs. Hamilton at Thru the Grapevine, Joan's husband at her home, the visiting secretary in the cemetery, the grocer and the banker from the old Queen's Hotel, Margaret on East John Street, the happy dog in the barn, Fred in Sheila Trecartin's store along with many other souls in Cookstown are visiting spirits.

A ghost, on the other hand, is a stuck earthbound spirit. They are departed souls who are not ready, willing or able to move on to the light after they have died. According to Karen Hollis of Om Times Magazine, there are 10 main reasons why a soul does not move into the light:

Unaware of Their Death: This can be common in the case of sudden or traumatic death. The individual had no time to prepare for death, and may be confused, fearful, or in shock. They can remain stuck at the site of the accident or incident that took their life. This is common on battlefields. Time stands still for ghosts. This may have been the case of Daniel at the hospital who was told to hide and stay put. He was lost, scared, confused and felt abandoned after his death. He may not have even realized he was dead and it took the intervention of his mother Rose to get him to move on.

Unfinished Business: We all have it, and if we carry it with us after death, it can keep us from moving into the Light. We all have to learn to let go at some point. This may have been the case of the pregnant Victorian woman who was pushed down the stairs by her father.

To Protect a Loved One: Some spirits have incredible

loyalty to those left behind. They feel obligated to continue their human role as protector. An example might be older siblings who looked after younger siblings. This is the case of the spirit dog that haunts the home on King Street. The dog is still guarding the house and the occupants. The dog may move on now that the threat in the garage has been removed.

Guilt: This is most common with suicides. A spirit, seeing the effect of their actions on loved ones may feel guilty about the choice they made. This is the case with both Margaret in Amy's house and the girl across the street from the ice cream parlour that committed suicide and has chosen to remain behind almost in punishment of what she did. It is also the case of the teenage boy who was in the Time's building. We have to stress that not all suicides remain earthbound. Most go to the light where they are loved and taken care of on the other side. If the old doctor who did careless surgery is still haunting his old home on Elizabeth Street, it may be the result of guilt. Certainly, it would be the case of the father of "Catherine" if he did push his daughter down the stairs.

Obsession or Love of another Living Soul: The inability to let go of, or harboring anger at, someone who is still alive, can keep a spirit from going on with their journey. Even a great love for someone can keep a spirit from moving on as they do not want to leave without them. This is the case of the little boy who drowned and is waiting for his older sister that he loves and possibly the case of the little girl who died of a sickness at the old Chestnut Inn and was looking for her mother. This could be the case of the psychiatric patient in the hospital who may have been angry at the doctor and staff at the hospital and would not move on until he was released through an exorcism. This may even be the case of Jonathan or Robert in the barn who was not obsessed with a person but with his coach house and material goods.

Feeling forced to stay by Another Ghost: This is not possible because every spirit has free will. It is possible that another spirit who had control over a newly deceased person is perceived to still have that power. An example would be an abusive man who dies before his wife. If she believes in death that the ghost of her husband has control over her, that perception can hold her back from the light.

Not Wanting to Face Someone Who Has Already Passed On: Just as we can be afraid to face someone in life whom we feel we have let down in some way or are scared of, so too can that fear be a powerful trap for the spirit to remain on the earth plane. Could this be the plight of the lady on the stairs?

Don't Believe in Life after Death: If one has no belief in a place to go after death, they may simply remain a wandering spirit.

Not Understanding That Existence Does Not End: Some spirits realize they are dead and in spirit form, but become fearful that leaving the earth plane will mean they cease to exist. The task here is to let go of the ego. This may have been the case of the little girl in the cemetery. She was aware she was dead but either didn't know how to move on or didn't want to because she may have been scared that she would no longer exist if she left the cemetery.

Fear of Judgment: If there is a place of Light, there also must be a place of Darkness. The fear that one might end up in darkness is powerful enough to keep one earthbound. We have a sense that the malicious, aggressive man who threatened Gary in his garage may be afraid to leave the earth plane because he is afraid of going somewhere darker than his creepy basement.

As Karen Hollis states, "In all cases, nothing binds a spirit to the earth plane except their own perception or emotional state, which they willingly choose".

According to Jane Ross who wrote the book, "I See Dead People", ghosts are everywhere and look just like you or I. They are transparent and are still holding onto their last physical space. They are physically dead, yet their spirit is unable to transition. There are millions of them, according to Jane, and they roam the earth most of the time feeling lost, confused, lonely, puzzled and searching for someone to finally notice and acknowledge their presence, talk to them and give them the answers to the questions they keep asking like, "Where Am I?" Many ghosts do not know they are dead, or if they do know, many are in denial of that fact.

If you think you have a ghost in your home or store or building, there are several things you can do to help them transition to the light. Ask Archangel Michael or the angels to bring the soul to the light or call on the loved ones of the soul to bring them into the light. Angels respect our free will on earth and will only intervene if asked. You can also light a white candle and tell the soul to go to the light. Call a medium like Sheila Trecartin who can talk to the ghost and help them to move on. Rescue mediums can reassure a soul that they won't be punished if they transition to the light and they can address their other fears and let them know they will be just fine if they leave the earth plane.

If you are dealing with a dark and angry spirit, which is not as common, you may need to have an exorcism performed. Nothing worked with the psychiatric patient at the old hospital so Gerry and Mardi finally had to have an exorcism. That angry spirit is now gone and at peace. The hostile spirit on the other side of Gary's garage might also require an exorcism to make him go. Certainly, the dark entity in the basement of the house Courtney lived in would require an exorcism to remove it from the house.

In the majority of cases, ghosts are just troubled, sad, lost, lonely or confused souls who need a little love or helping hand to move them on their way to the other side. They are just people and often our fear of ghosts and spirit stems more from our own imagination then anything the ghost or spirit is actually doing. We are afraid of the unknown.

We are afraid of souls we can't see. We are afraid of things that go bump in the night even if that bump is just departed grandma or grandpa moving around the house. In some cases, like Courtney's the fear is very real and justified, but in most cases, it is not.

Spirit Hitchikers
How to Protect Yourself

When Amy moved into her house on King Street in Cookstown, her abilities to sense energy found it to be calm and peaceful. She sensed there was a spirit who liked to frequent the pantry but that spirit welcomed her family. No real strange occurrences came about until Amy started to co-write this book. What Amy and Cate did not realize at the time is that when investigating a haunted location, you can pick up spirit hitchhikers who will come home with you if you do not protect yourself first. Spirits followed both Amy and Cate home.

In Amy's case, she had been investigating a haunted building earlier in the day. Right before settling down for the night she happened to open her eyes in the darkness and found a strange man looking right at her. The man disappeared within seconds. It was unsettling to see this stranger.

Another incident involved her make-up flying off a shelf in her closet in the middle of the night. Nothing had ever moved off that shelf in the past so it was very odd and disturbing.

Cate has a young son who can see spirit. She found out he had this gift when he was six years old and he told her about the spirits he saw. He spoke of a man in an orange t-shirt who didn't know he was dead and a woman in a yellow print dress in their living room. He spoke of shadow figures and grey figures. Cate watched one day as her son ran around the house chasing the family cat. All of a sudden he let out a yell and stopped running. Cate said he was definitely startled by something. Her son told her he almost ran into the back of a ghost boy who disappeared down the hall. Cate later found out that her house was not haunted but the street she lives on was haunted. She was informed by three different mediums that there was a portal on the street. Ghosts come and go through it and will walk through her home and the homes of other people nearby. Cate and her son are sensitive so they sense or even see the ghosts. Others on the street who are not sensitive have no idea what is going on.

After Cate investigated a haunted building, the spirit of a Victorian woman followed Cate home. For several nights, Cate's son described a woman in a long dress who appeared by the window of the bedroom and walked to the bedroom door and then disappeared. It scared her son and he had to sleep with the lights on after that. The situation made Cate call Sheila. Sheila confirmed that a ghost woman had followed her home and she told Cate how to make the spirit leave. After that, they were told to surround themselves in a white light and say, "I take only what is mine" after they left a haunted building to prevent any more unwanted hitchhikers. Cate's son has not had any more sightings of the Victorian woman in the middle of the night and Amy's house is calm and peaceful once more.

If you ghost hunt, do protect yourself so you don't end up with an attachment or end up bringing unwanted strangers into your own home. You can use the technique Sheila Trecartin described above. Visualize yourself surrounded in the white light of God's protection and say "I only take what is mine" when you exit a haunted building or site. If you have a hard time visualizing, ask to be covered in the white light of God's protection. A single prayer for protection from anything that might harm you or attach to you or follow you home is equally effective. Invoking the name of Archangel Michael is something ghost hunters frequently do especially if they feel they are in the presence of a dark or angry spirit or feel threatened in any way. Old jails or old psychiatric wards, for example, are not places you would want to investigate unless you were protected. Some ghost hunters bring holy water, rosaries, a cross or other religious artifacts with them to these places.

Many ghost hunters think it is wise to bless the house or building, its inhabitants and themselves at the end of an investigation. Saging and allowing the smoke to permeate each room is a good way of expelling any negative energy from a home or building. The use of wind chimes, angelic items, essential oils, incense, flowers, crystals, healing sounds and music all help to keep the atmosphere positive.

Ghost hunting or going on a ghost walk can be entertaining and interesting but it is always best to be aware and know what you are doing before you participate in any event involving spirits.

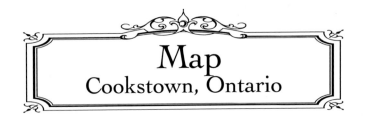

Map
Cookstown, Ontario

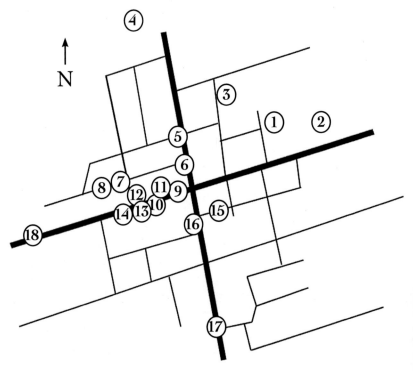

1. Curling Club
2. Cemetery
3. Old Hospital
4. Antique Barn
5. Ghost Dog House
6. Sheila's
7. Old School
8. Train Station
9. Ice Cream Store
10. Chestnut Inn
11. Cabo
12. Timepiece
13. Queen's Hotel Area
14. Thru The Grapevine
15. South Simcoe Theatre
16. Amy's House
17. Mr. Cooke's House
18. Joan's House

If you have a ghost story that you would like to share about Cookstown, please contact us and it could be put in subsequent editions of this book.
Your story can be e-mailed to Amy at amben@hot-mail.com or to Cate at catecrow63@yahoo.ca or you can mail in your story to Amy Woodcock c/o PO Box 1355, Cookstown, Ontario L0L 1L0